# Christian Faith
## and
# Environmental Stewardship

# Christian Faith and Environmental Stewardship

Theological Foundations for Creation Care

DANIEL K. LAGAT

RESOURCE *Publications* • Eugene, Oregon

CHRISTIAN FAITH AND ENVIRONMENTAL STEWARDSHIP
Theological Foundations for Creation Care

Copyright © 2019 Daniel K. Lagat. All rights reserved. Except for brief quotations in critical publications or reviews, no part of this book may be reproduced in any manner without prior written permission from the publisher. Write: Permissions, Wipf and Stock Publishers, 199 W. 8th Ave., Suite 3, Eugene, OR 97401.

Resource Publications
An Imprint of Wipf and Stock Publishers
199 W. 8th Ave., Suite 3
Eugene, OR 97401

www.wipfandstock.com

PAPERBACK ISBN: 978-1-5326-7000-8
HARDCOVER ISBN: 978-1-5326-7001-5
EBOOK ISBN: 978-1-5326-7002-2

Manufactured in the U.S.A. 03/12/19

*To my sweetheart, Zippy
And the children we have been blessed with,
I treasure your support and grace;
you all have been like jewels for me.*

# Contents

*Preface* | ix
*Acknowledgement* | xi
*Abbreviations* | xiii

Chapter One
Introduction: Christianity and Environment | 1

Chapter Two
The Position of a Christian as a Steward | 7

Chapter Three
Environmental Adversity in Kenya: Opportunity to Change | 24

Chapter Four
Christian Worldview of Environmental Stewardship | 43

Chapter Five
Call for a Christian to Participate
in Environmental Stewardship | 66

Chapter Six
The Conserving Church in Kenya | 89

*Bibliography* | 109

# Preface

ADAPTATION IS ONE KEY factor that determine survival of living things on earth. Extinction usually occurs to living species who are unable to adapt to the changing environment on earth. The recent changes in the world climate means that several species will go extinct, especially those unwilling to adapt to changes. Christian religion has been the power behind remarkable transformation in many countries. Christian faith generally nurtures people to adopt progressive mindset, a necessary component to successful acceptance of change. Christian faith has been instrumental in the response against hunger, poverty, diseases, et cetera. In responding to Climate Change and environmental concerns, which are the world's most pressing issues now, however, religion has generally been silent, or unnoticed. Although it may appear that Christians have not done much to respond to environmental concerns, some denominations are exerting noticeable and exemplary efforts. The aim of this book is to present important principles needed for a Christian to exert necessary effort to care for the creation. The information presented include initiatives closely tied to the unique combination of Christian disciplines of prayer, giving, and fellowships; with serious monitoring of environmental adaptation initiatives, evaluation, and accountability mechanisms. It is envisaged that this combination helps Christians to be relevant, especially in helping a community to adapt and remain resilient. The book also presents worldview aspects that play crucial role in the transformation of Christians to adopt change. When Christians thus go to

## Preface

their farms, they do so with an attitude of reverence, as though they were into a place of worship. Furthermore, it was found that CIM initiatives transformed people and developed in them a culture of hard work and productive living; so that the people overcame the need to depend on relief food. Readers of this book will appreciate the workable theology of environmental management discussed, which includes proper perspective of environment, biblical work ethic, and accountability systems. Christians in Kenya can benefit from this book as it provides practical options where they could contribute to environmental adaptation.

# Acknowledgement

CREATION CARE AND ENVIRONMENTAL stewardship thinking comes out of my experience working as a project manager at Care of Creation Kenya, where I was blessed with a rare opportunity of reading books, interacting with leading scholars and creation care leaders, attending conferences, and participating in creation care meetings. I am immensely grateful to Craig Sorley who motivated me to think about the role of the Church in environmental stewardship, and who gave me books and other resources that were helpful in the framework and literature review that guided this work. At Care of Creation Kenya, I got the privilege of meeting Professor Calvin DeWitt, Rev Edward Brown, Ben Lowe, Dr. Dave Bookless, Dr Roger Sharland, among others. These leading scholars shaped my thinking and helped me conceive the problem affecting creation care in a better way. I am very grateful to United States International University and Moi University for guidance in higher education, and specifically in the area of religion and environment, which was my doctoral research. Great thanks go to Professor Eunice Kamaara and Professor Joseph Koech for their close supervision, constructive criticism, and encouragement throughout the writing of this thesis. For me, they remain more than just supervisors; they have been mentors and friends. Professor William (Bill) Cavanaugh and Professor Stan Chu Ilo offered books to read, encouragement, and very helpful critiques, which have shaped this book to a meaningful extent. I am sincerely thankful to the research fellowship given by the Centre for World

*Acknowledgement*

Catholicism and Intercultural Theology (CWCIT) at Depaul University, Illinois, where I got a precious time to look through my work in detail, and an ample time to read materials available at Depaul Library between June and August 2018. I am also indebted to Partnership for African Social and Governance Research (PASGR) intensive training on Advanced Research Design, Survey, Ethnography, Multi-Method Research, Engendering Research, and Research Ethics modules, which transformed my understanding of research and scholarship, especially in relation to public policy. I benefited from the Association of Commonwealth Universities summer program at Bath Spa University in August 2017. I was also privileged to attend a Religion and Science course at Faraday Institute, Cambridge University in June-July 2017.

# Abbreviations

AIDS Acquired Immune-Deficiency Syndrome

CIM: Christian Impact Mission

CTC: Cape Town Confession

DoA: Department of Agriculture

DRSRS: Department of Resource Surveys and Remote Sensing

FGD: Focus Group Discussion

GOK: Government of Kenya

HIV: Human Immuno-Deficiency Virus

KNA: Kenya National Archives

KFWG: Kenya Forest Working Group

MDG: Millennium Development Goals

NEMA: National Environment Management Authority

NIV: New International Version

NGO: Non-Governmental Organization

OMO: Operation *Mwolyo* Out (*Mwolyo* is a Kamba word for relief food)

UN: United Nations

US: United States

UNEP: United Nations Environmental Program

CHAPTER ONE

# Introduction
*Christianity and Environment*

The main ingredients of an environmental ethic are caring about the planet and all of its inhabitants, allowing unselfishness to control the immediate self-interest that harms others, and living each day so as to leave the lightest possible footprints on the planet.

—ROBERT CAHN

The culture-ideology of consumerism proclaims, literally, that the meaning of life is to be found in the things that we possess. To consume, therefore, is to be fully alive, and to remain fully alive we must consume.

—LESLIE. SKLAIR, SOCIOLOGY OF THE GLOBAL-SYSTEM, 47–48

THE ROLE OF RELIGION in human development has been a subject of scrutiny for many scholars. According to Gerrie Ter Haar and Stephen Ellis the question of whether religion has an impact in the development of any nation has been answered in the affirmative.[1] The United Nations Development Program asserts that the process of human development should "at least create an environment for people, individually and collectively, to develop to their full potential and to have a reasonable chance of leading productive and creative lives that they value."[2] Religion contributes in creating this environment in a variety of ways, as will be discussed in this book. Although in some countries in Africa religion has been seen to support terrorism and, in the process, hampering development, this has not tainted Christianity in Kenya in any significant way. Religion has contributed immensely in the development of health sector, education, and cultivation of the culture of hard work. In Kenya, many schools were originally founded by churches, institutions that have produced the current leaders in the society. Christianity has been energetic in humanitarian activities, peacekeeping, HIV/AIDS response and other similar roles.

According to Presbyterian Eco Justice Task Force, far more disastrous than the problems that the Church has handled in the past, are issues of climate change and environmental degradation.[3] The Task Force observes:

> Thus far, the Church has been more responsive to the threat from armed violence than to the threat from the unsustainable management of human fertility and human demands. There is, after all, a long tradition of concern about welfare and the counterproductive consequences from growing arsenals of deadly weapons. Now we must grapple with the new idea that the impact of human numbers and human interventions may be more than nature can endure- and that this has profound implications for achieving distributive justice.[4]

1. Haar & Ellis, The Role of Religion in Development, 1.
2. United Nations Development Program, Human Development Report, 1.
3. Presbyterian Eco-Justice Task Force, *Keeping and Healing the Creation*, 19.
4. Ibid.

*Introduction*

Eric Rignot and Pannir Kanagaratnam in reference to climatic change, observe that global impacts in areas such as damage of the ozone layer have left consequences such as enormous temperatures on earth that have made some parts of the universe gradually uninhabitable.[5] As a result, heads of states have often converged to deliberate on measures that need to be taken to reverse the situation, or at least contain it.

In Africa, climate change damages have left devastating effects, especially because in most parts of Africa, the economy is largely nature-based, and because Africans are less able to cope or adapt to climate change than other continents.[6] The fact that Africa has contributed the least in inducing climate change makes the circumstance an unfair treatment to the continent. Reid Basher and Sálvano Briceño contend:

> Africa's vulnerability is partly driven by unfortunate geography, where the physical effects of climate change are likely to be among the most severe on the planet. It is also largely the result of the low adaptive capacity of many African states, which is a product of problems in their economies, health-care and education systems, infrastructure, and governance.[7]

As noted above, Africa's vulnerability is closely tied to desertification in the continent. Deserts, arid, and semi-arid regions are possibly the most food insecure places. The effect of the advancing desert from Somalia, which is sweeping through the entire north and eastern Kenya is threatening the people living in the country. While education and development are the priorities of many countries in the world, Kenya is facing a situation where food and water for domestic use become the main concern, for they are perpetually becoming unavailable. Kenya's five major water towers are on the verge of collapse, with snowy caps of mountains such as Kilimanjaro, Kenya, Ruwenzori, and Elgon, now melting at a

---

5. Rignot & Kanagaratnam, Changes in Greenland Ice Sheet, 21.
6. Luganda, Africa and Climate Change, 44.
7. Basher & Briceño, Climate and Disaster Risk Reduction in Africa, 270.

rate never recorded before in history.[8] According to Russell *et al* (2009), these mountains have lost over 80 per cent of their surface area between 1900 and 1990, and now only a total of less than 10km$^2$ is remaining.

The impact of climate and environmental deterioration means that Kenya has become and may continue to be food insecure. Jessica Leber notes: "experts predict climate change will increase Kenya's already tough food security challenges."[9] The country now imports some of its food, yet the people are poor, and the government economy is majorly supported by taxes. It is gradually becoming normal to see people in many areas walking for long distances in search of water, food and pasture, sometimes moving with children and animals. In many parts of the country, violence has erupted several times because communities are fighting for natural resources such as water and pasture, which are now limited. Even the elaborate traditional mechanisms for coping with a harsh environment have been overwhelmed and that life for many millions has become a "little more than a form of chronic disaster."[10]

Prevalent poverty and dependence on rain-fed agriculture has further exacerbated vulnerability in Kenya. Even in the rare instance of normal rainfall, Africa fails to produce enough food to meet its needs, leading to chronic food insecurity and overdependence on emergency food relief (as cited in Luganda, 2008). In fact, the World Bank estimates that by 2080, "African agricultural output could fall by 16 percent."[11] Farmers are the first and directly affected in the country. Jessica Leber observes that the "rising global temperatures are ending what little predictability farmers could count on in the past. . . Farmers only have one chance to time the planting right. If the rains fail to arrive on time, the crop dies, and with it, so does the bulk of their annual income" (Ibid). Pat-

8. Luganda, Africa and Climate Change, 34.

9. Leber How Farmers in Kenya Might Adapt to Climate Change, 25.

10. Presbyterian Eco-Justice Task Force, *Keeping and Healing the Creation*, 8.

11. Leber, How Farmers in Kenya Might Adapt to Climate Change, 2.

*Introduction*

rick Luganda observes: "because farmers and rain-fed agriculture are critically important to food security and African economies in general, helping them adapt is a prime focus of many adaptation projects."[12] Jikun Huang, Carl Pray, and Scott Rozelle observe that the "struggle for a better life" in the developing world, depends on the abundance of affordable food.[13] They further contend:

> One of the great challenges of the coming decades will be to produce the food and fibre that is needed to feed and clothe those in the poorer parts of the world. And although from some perspectives this seems like an impossible task — in the same way that it must have to the doomsday forecasters since the days of Malthus — there are many reasons to believe it can be achieved.[14]

This shows that, for a country like Kenya, which is classified as developing nation, food for citizens continue to become a major struggle. This struggle should become a priority, not just for the government, but also for non-state agencies, for example the Church. The Church in Kenya plays a central role in mobilization of citizens, and in behavior change.

The Cornwall Declaration, jointly declared by the Church leaders in 2004 at Cornwall, lamented the 'conspicuous' passiveness of the Church on environmental management. They observe that many Christians have been passive on the area, and some have even been seen to use Christianity to justify degradation of the environment. Ruth Goring Stewart, although not entirely agreeing with Lynn White Jr who sensationally accused Christianity of being the most anthropocentric and environment-insensitive religion, Stewart still thinks that Christian religion has some blame to take.[15] She notes:

> The Church is certainly not blameless. Some Christians have indeed used the words have dominion and subdue

---

12. Luganda, Africa and Climate Change, 8.
13. Huang, Pray, & Rozelle, "Enhancing the Crops to Feed the Poor," 678.
14. Ibid.
15. Stewart, *Environmental Stewardship*, 12.

# Christian Faith and Environmental Stewardship

from the King James Version of Genesis to justify exploitative practices. Even when secular movements arose to call Western society to a new sense of environmental responsibility, the church was all too slow to respond.[16]

Stewart's discussion apportions blame to Christians in history that either exhibited 'domination' and destructive attitudes throughout the world and in history, or gave the behavior a blind eye, because of their theological orientation. Christians who moved from Europe to America were recorded to have cut down trees, rolling them over Amazon and Mississippi rivers for free transport, in the long run spoiling a lot of them. Similar behaviors have been noted in other places of the world, where Christians demonstrated exploitative behavior that was detrimental to the environment. Stewart posits that the right interpretation of Genesis 1–2 does not in any way propagate exploitation. Interpreting the words properly gives the meaning that Christians are to care for the environment.[17] Nonetheless, some Christians used this wrong theological position to cause environmental degradation, most of the time thinking they were performing their mandate. This therefore is a case example where the Church would be considered to have set the wrong example. Edward Brown says the solution to the environmental crisis lies in the right approach.[18] The approach that is sustainable should be theologically sound, scientifically informed and implemented by a community of redeemed people acting out of love for God and for each other.

This book thus seeks to present reflections of how Christian faith can support environmental stewardship.

---

16. Ibid.
17. Ibid.
18. Brown, *Our Father's World*, 79.

CHAPTER TWO

# The Position of a Christian as a Steward

We have been given the earth to live, not on, but with and from, and only on the condition that we care properly for it.

—WENDEL BERRY (DAVIS, E. F, 2009, P. IX)

## INTRODUCTION

WHEN GOD CREATED A human being, he also gave them his image and likeness. The image and likeness of God positioned a human being higher in the creation order, making them "a little lower than the angels."[1] Man became of the class of God in some way, with authority, but also with responsibility. Edward Brown asserts that Humanity has been given a unique position and a special status.[2] They were created to act as true representatives of God in the garden. A human being is an incarnate creature, with a living soul, which makes him very different from the other creatures, but gives

1. Psalms 8:5
2. Brown, *When Heaven and Nature Sing*, 49.

him the responsibility over the other creatures. This awesome responsibility comes with authority but also with consequences. In a world that reflects God's goals, every person will understand that he or she shares responsibility for ruling God's world and will have the opportunity to exercise that responsibility in his or her own life. When God thus tells Adam to have dominion and subdue, it was because man was acting out of the privileged and delegated responsibility. Stan Chu Ilo notes that, the fact that Adam and Eve were created in the image of God "is the greatest evidence that the human person is to exercise dominion over the earth with wisdom and love."[3] The Fall of man however, which brought the death of relationships between God and man, also invalidated human ability to act fully as agents carrying the image and the likeness of God, and this severely compromised human ability to exercise control over the environment. The death of Christ on the cross, which was God's intervention to redeem humanity, became an avenue also in which humans can have their image and likeness to God being restored. A Christians therefore has a unique role, more than any other person, to perform God-given tasks of environmental stewardship.

It is important at the onset of this chapter to define the meaning of stewardship as is understood in this realm and discipline.

## WHAT IS STEWARDSHIP

Edward Brown defines a steward as someone who takes care of something on behalf of someone else.[4] A steward then becomes a special owner, exercising the authority specially given to him by the owner, to act as though he was the owner, for the benefit of the owner, who will call him to account every act and decision. As pertaining environmental management, stewardship is the understanding that God did make the world for himself, but has assigned humanity the responsibility to care, having in mind the

3. Ilo, *The Church and Development in Africa*, 78.
4. Brown, *Our Father's World*, 33.

## The Position of a Christian as a Steward

fact that God still needs his world in the future for his own worship, and for the people that will be there then. According to the Brundtland Report the concept of sustainable developments can be defined as "development that meets the needs of the present without compromising the ability of future generations to meet their own needs."[5] This concern for others is central to Christ's teaching of loving one's neighbor.

The meaning of stewardship is elaborated further by Calvin DeWitt who perceives it through the lens of *oikonomia*, the economy of the house. Dewitt affirms that the word stewardship circumscribes relationship between human economies and the economy of God's wider creation. The word 'economy,' comes from the Greek word *oikonomia*, and means "management of the household."[6] This also requires an understanding of the entire creation as a household of God, where all people are housed. It is an imaginary house, where all people live together sharing resources and shelter. Stewardship in this perspective is the use and care for the household on behalf of God, who put up the household and all its inhabitants. This understanding also impacts the view of economy. Endeavours to build the economy should not compromise the condition of the household or go contrary to the intention of the creator.[7] Having defined the meaning of stewardship in the biblical sense, we need now to discuss the person who is described as a steward in the Bible.

Christian perspective of the meaning of stewardship must also include the application of the life of Jesus on earth, to determine the meaning and purpose of stewardship in the modern world. While drawing conclusions from the context of the life of Jesus, Vernon Visick argues that "Jesus' time was permeated with general awareness of human dependence upon, and interdependence with nature."[8] The people in Jesus' time thus had a way of caring for the

---

5. World Commission on Environment and Development, "Report," 1.
6. DeWitt, *Caring for Creation*, 33.
7. Ibid.
8. Visick, *The Environment and the Christian*, 97.

creation, and the general principle of stewardship was worked out in terms of three subsidiary principles summarised as:

(1) *Baltashit* (do not destroy);

(2) The prohibition against inflicting *za'arbaaleihayyim* (pain of living things); and

(3) The keeping of the Sabbath, Sabbath year and even the Jubilee.[9]

According to Visick, stewardship involved constant application of these three principles in life. All activities revolved around not destroying, not inflicting pain, and Sabbath rest. Visick thus deduces that Jesus lived in an environment where the law and the culture supported environmental stewardship. The law gave the people opportunities to make choices that were right, and that honored God. Although no record shows directly how Jesus acted towards the environment, this argument by Visick, based on literature about the Jewish way of life during the time of Jesus, is logically valid. It could be argued thus, that Jesus' attitude towards law, Visick adds, "Was that of constant application and reapplication, as the situation demanded."[10]

## THE PERSON, STEWARD

Edward Brown asserts that Christians need to care for the environment more than anyone else, because they have relationships with the creator.[11] The proper approach to creation care should be implemented by a community of redeemed people, who understand the love for God and the love for neighbor. The bar of performance for the Church of course, is higher than is expected of others. The First epistle of John 3:5 state that anyone who claims to know Jesus Christ should also walk in his light. As will be discussed later, Jesus is creator, integrator, and reconciler. Ironically, many who call on

9. Ibid., 99.
10. Ibid., 99.
11. Brown, *Our Father's World*, 79.

## The Position of a Christian as a Steward

his name, sometimes abuse, neglect, or even do not give care to God's creation. This is contradicting the very nature of a Christian, honoring God the creator verbally, yet harming God's work practically; praising God from whom all blessings flow yet diminishing and destroying God's creatures on earth; learning in the Church that God created all things in good condition and destroying that which was created as good. Cal DeWitt summarizes this contradiction precisely: The pieces of this puzzle do not fit! One piece says, "We honor the Great Master!" The other piece says, "We despise his great master pieces!" (DeWitt 1998, 16).

Christians sometimes argue that they are not the right people to serve God in environmental stewardship because they are weak financially, or academically. God however still calls and equips them in a miraculous way. The people that have served God successfully are not the people that had resources in abundance; they were the people that served God with faithfulness. In Exodus, God calls Moses and sends him to Egypt. Moses however feels incapable and asks God to send someone else. In response, God asks Moses what he was holding in his hand. God wanted Moses to realize that whatever little resources are at our disposal, God can use them to do great things. For us, it is a lesson not to despise small resources that we have. He must have also learned another lesson that little resources like the staff, if used well, can help us achieve greater goals such as delivering the people who are in bondage. Usually, people are waiting for "others" to do the will of God. People want God to send someone else. Yet everybody is gifted with resources such as hands, mind, land, rain, rivers, manure, ant hill soil *et cetera*, that may seem to be of little help, but when used appropriately could bring more results. When Christians wait upon the Lord, they begin to see how the all-sufficient God provides for them. God's favour comes to us with an ability to create wealth.

The steward understands the master and is joyful about the roles he is given. Edward Brown discusses this principle of loving and valuing things that were made by the people we hold in high esteem. He observes:

## Christian Faith and Environmental Stewardship

> If I can place a high price on things that have a little or no intrinsic value simply because they were made by one of my children, how much more ought I to value and care for this amazing world God made, this world that is precious because He made it and that represents an excellence and beauty far beyond anything that any of us begin to comprehend, let alone make on our own.[12]

Craig Sorley asserts:

> We can all agree that there is a standard we must uphold when we are in possession of something that does not belong to us, an obligation to respect and care for something that is owned by another. We can also agree that we should uphold this standard whether we borrow something from our friend, our neighbor, or from a prominent leader in our country. In every case, we should return that item to its owner in the same condition as when we borrowed it. Better yet, to show our appreciation, we may even take steps to repair or improve that item so that the owner can enjoy receiving it back in even better condition.[13]

A steward understands that God has given instruction on how to care for his earth. Many have even labored to show the scriptural support for that. But has God prescribed ways to care for creation? Ken Gnanakan asserts that because God deeply loves his creation gift, He has given instructions and practical commands of how he expects his stewards to take care of it (Gnanakan 2004, 58). Some ways of doing stewardship, as suggested by scholars such as Vernon J. Ehlers, offer ways such as becoming well educated in matters to do with environment, making environmental policies, becoming politically active, working with others to be effective, and becoming sympathetic to the environment.[14] This book discusses various roles how stewardship can be exercised in Kenya. In

---

12. Brown, *Our Father's World*, 41.
13. Sorley, *Christ and Creation*, 70.
14. Ehlers, *Caring for the Creation*, 94–98.

fact, in chapter six, I point out practical steps I propose to be done by churches to realize environmental stewardship success.

## SUCCESSFUL STEWARDSHIP

The parable of the talents in Matthew 25:11–30 is a story of what Jesus will do during judgement. When Jesus gave this story, he wanted his followers to know that being "the servants" of the king also means having the privilege and the opportunity to receive "talents" from the king for trading to make profits. Jesus also wanted his followers to know that the king (Jesus himself) would be happy upon his return to meet his servants having made profit from the talents they were given. The servant in the parable who did not make profits, was "thrown outside, where there was gnashing of teeth and wailing." The message there is that the responsibility of making profits also come with accountability. Christians who are God's ministers on earth now have been positioned in this daunting task, where they either make profits with the talents they have been given by God, or suffer the hard consequence of having "even what else they have" being taken away from them, and then being thrown out into the "outside, where there will be wailing and gnashing of teeth." The success of the stewards can be attributed majorly to their awareness of their master's intention for the talents, their effort to increase and multiply the talents given, and their excitement in accounting for the talents given. The entire chapter revolves around these three secrets of success. We will first discuss awareness of the master's intentions as being instrumental for the success of stewardship.

## a) Awareness of God's Intention for the Earth

The importance of understanding God's intention for the earth is paramount and helps in the determination of necessary actions that human beings can or should do. This can be related to understanding the mind behind an art or a design, why something was brought to existence. The successful stewards in the parable that Jesus shared, demonstrated that they understood why they were given the talents, and even went ahead to show that they did what was expected. A Christian too, who understands God's intentions for the earth, will most likely succeed. A good steward would first appreciate that whatever talents they have, belongs to the master, and not them. The entire environment is God's creation. It is not just nature. It is a resource belonging to God but given to humans as a talent. Psalm 24:1-2; and Psalm 50:9-11 indicate:

> The earth is the Lord's and everything in it, all the world and all who live in it; for he founded it upon the seas and established it upon the waters... I have no need of a bull from your stall or of goats from your pens, for every animal of the forest is mine, and the cattle on a thousand hills. I know every bird in the mountain, and the creatures of the field are mine (NIV).

God clearly demonstrates the fact that the resources are His, especially land in the Old Testament. The things that people tend to think of as our "resources" are actually elements of the creation belonging to God. God the owner gives them graciously to his people, not to a few capitalists. Not to a few owners for their own selfish pleasure. The resource was given to all people and all generations for their sustenance. The Presbyterian Eco-Justice Task Force opines that "our access to these gifts is comparable to the provision in Roman law called "usufruct": the right to enjoy all the advantages derivable from the use of something belonging to another, on condition that the substance of the thing not be destroyed or injured."[15]

In Leviticus (25:23), God tells the Israelites that 'the land was his, and that Israelites were but aliens and tenants. In Jeremiah (2:7; 16:18), God is clear about the fact that land was his. Israelites only received what was apportioned to them by the owner. In 2 Samuel the Hebrew word *nahalah* is used (2 Samuel 20:19, 21:3), meaning landed property apportioned to an individual. God gave

15. Presbyterian Eco-Justice Task Force, *Keeping and Healing the Creation*, 5.

## The Position of a Christian as a Steward

the land to Israel, but it was still His land (Deuteronomy 25:23) and therefore, no one was free to do as he liked.[16] In Deuteronomy 11 God confirms that the land which was being given to Israelites was better in form and produce, and that they would continue benefiting from the land as long as they obeyed God. In fact, God makes it clear that if they were disobedient, they would be thrown out of the land. God gives it for their use, their livelihood, their enjoyment –not as their exclusive property to be exploited selfishly but as a trust to be developed with care. The land was supposed to be used as an instrument of justice and community. Reading Deuteronomy 11 brings out an opinion that land represented wealth, freedom, abundance, and fulfilment for the Hebrew people in contrast to the affliction, toil, and option of their enslavement in Egypt. The condition that Israelites were to enjoy the land if they remained obedient to God, confirmed clearly that God owned the land; and that he just had apportioned a share to the Israelites. Therefore, this land was a resource, a talent, being given to servants, for enjoyment and use, but continued being God's. Any treatment needed to conform to the expectation of the owner.[17]

As discussed above, stewardship is taking care of something that belongs to another. The steward does not own what is being cared for. Environmental stewardship is caring for what belongs to God. Christians, who in this case are stewards, only are authorized to make intelligent decisions on behalf of God, the actual owner, in a way to best reflect His wishes. God's intentions for his gift have been provided in the Bible. The clearest intention in my opinion, is that the environment was created so that it can worship God.

## Creation for God's worship

One of the profound motivations for environmental stewardship I have found, is the awareness that the environment, God's creation, exists to worship God. Edward Brown avers that the biggest reason

16. Gnanakan, *Responsible Stewardship of God's Creation*, 61.
17. Presbyterian Eco-Justice Task Force, *Keeping and Healing the Creation*, 33.

for caring for God's creation is not more about the extent of the severity of the environmental crisis, nor the number of people affected or their ultimate future. He says the main reason is God himself. God created everything for his own purpose, praise and worship. Brown says, Christians care because they know and love the owner.[18] This owner also delights in the works of his hands. Craig Sorley observes:

> One of the pleasures of being an artist or craftsman is step back after many hours of work, and to enjoy a sense of fulfilment in a job well done. The degree of satisfaction experienced is directly proportional to the degree of excellence seen in the final product... Delight in a job well done is excellence, the final product is magnificence beyond human understanding, and so is the proportion of God's pleasure when He pronounces it to be *"very good."*[19]

In other words, God enjoys seeing the excellence of his creation speaking forth His excellence. The universe is a lavish demonstration of the incredible, incomparable, unimaginable exuberance and the greatness of God.[20] Stewardship of creation is therefore about the desire to worship God and to lead what God has creation in worship to Him. While addressing the Wheaton Summit in 2007, Fred Van Dyke posited: "although the stewardship we offer is intended to bring benefit to God's creation, the offering itself is one that we direct toward almighty God, the creator of heaven and earth, and Jesus Christ, his only Son, our Lord."[21] Jonathan Edwards further posits:

> We have shown that the Son of God created the world for this very end, to communicate Himself in an image of His own Excellency... When we behold the light and brightness of the sun, the golden edges of an evening cloud, or the beauteous rainbow, we behold the adumbrations of

18. Brown, *Our Father's World*, 32.
19. Sorley, *Christ and Creation*, 50.
20. Piper, *The Pleasures of God*, 93.
21. van Dyke in Lowe, 166.

*The Position of a Christian as a Steward*

his glory and goodness, and in the blue sky, of His mildness and gentleness.[22]

Since the entire creation was created by God and for God, caring for creation can only be to facilitate that. Brown opines that the task of mobilizing the Church to respond to the environmental crisis needs to begin with worship.[23] The attitude of worship begins with a sense of wonder, realizing what God has done already. Dyke and others ask, "Is there not a sense in which we should remove our sandals, as Moses did in the desert because the ground is holy if God is there?"[24] This sense of wonder is what transforms a lot of attitudes, to see what God has done first, and be moved into the desire to treat it with respect. This of course is not in any way to suggest worshipping the creation, but to wonder at the creation, Christians think about the designer. God's creation is a holy ground and all of it is "worship space. It must be respected and cared for.[25] In his book *When Heaven and Nature Sing* (2012) Brown envisions a future where human beings will understand their roles in creation care, and that each will seek to please the Lord. The vision is realistic, as it is based on realistic efforts by ordinary human beings who have a positive world view. His argument is that in a world that reflects God's goals, in a world where humanity is aware of who the Master is, all human activity will be done in such a way that they proclaim God's name by working in harmony with and contributing to the flourishing of human and non-human creation. So, creation exists for God's glory, to worship God.

## Creation for humanity's benefit

God created the earth for His own glory, but also for humanity's benefit. This is the second fact, the second intention of God's creation, which Christians need to be aware of, in case they will be

22. Sorley, *Christ and Creation*, 38.
23. Brown, *Our Father's World*, 93.
24. van Dyke, Mahan, Sheldon, & Brand, *Redeeming Creation*, 16.
25. Brown, *Our Father's World*, 37.

successful to provide stewardship roles. In Calvin Institutes "the end for which all things were created [was] that none of the convenience and necessities of life might be wanting to men" (Calvin, Institutes of Christian Religion, Vol I, xiv 2; xiv 22. ). Since this seems to be God's original idea, to bring into existence resources that can benefit man too, it should be the desire of all stewards to see that that is accomplished. Although stewards do not ultimately own the property they care for, they are empowered to make intelligent decisions on behalf of God, the actual owner, in a way to best reflect his wishes. Stewardship therefore is the opportunity and responsibility to care and using the fruitfulness of creation for human sustenance and enjoyment.[26] In a way, when Christians become good stewards in this respect, they also demonstrate their love for their neighbours. Brown opines that there is no way a church can profess to love its neighbours, when they fail to care for the water and the trees that gives them life and enjoyment. Christians that are practicing good stewardship of commonly shared resources will usually be appreciated and respected together with their message.[27]

The Earth is equipped with fruitfulness and capacity to satisfy human needs due to its vast resources given by the designer, making it just the right gift for humanity. Although as the Acton Institute argue, work and intelligence are required to unleash the fruitfulness of the earth, the fact that the earth is endowed with those resources, for all needs and cravings, ranging from food, medicine, water, air, *et cetera*, care should be exercised to utilize rather than damage these resources.[28] The earth is also endowed with ability to rejuvenate itself. Unlike man made resources, such as machines, the earth has inherent capacity to rebuild itself after some resources have been harvested from it. For example, if you harvest some trees from a forest, and leave it for 50 years, when you come back, you find the forest thick again. Of course, the rate and success of rejuvenation depends on the extent of initial damage.

26. Lowe, *Green Revolution*, 42.
27. Brown, *Our Father's World*, 125.
28. Acton Institute, *Environmental Stewardship*, 7.

This shows some of God's intention for utilization of what God offered for human consumption: resources were meant for other generations to come. If everyone would carefully harvest what is just enough for use, and protect the remaining for others, the earth would be a never drying spring of resources.

Human lifestyle and practices have sometimes limited enjoyment of God's resources. The Presbyterian Eco-Justice Task Force assert that "the phenomenon of waste and pollution, as found in municipal waste management, chemical production, use, and disposal, and (it could be shown) the radioactive contamination associated with nuclear power and nuclear weapons," is largely a demonstration of unnecessary wasting of God's wealth and the irresponsible poisoning of human and nonhuman creatures. According to the Task Force, "the economic enterprise need not be so violent, or the enjoyment of a good life so dependent upon synthetic things."[29]

## Creation for Future Economic Benefit

The reason for environmental stewardship cannot end with human enjoyment here and now. It must be concerned with future generations too. God's intention was not just Adam the historical figure, but Adam the humanity. God had the humanity in mind, when he provided for *his* food, plants and animals in Genesis. Environmental stewardship therefore, includes activities that will make life on earth tomorrow, to be possible and better. Presbyterian Eco-Justice Task Force, (1989) argue that "the deeper insight behind recycling is not that it saves money but that it keeps for the community the materials that still are good for something- for manufacturing, for composting, for saving energy- because to treat these things as 'waste' would really be wasteful."[30] The concern should not end with self. It should put into consideration the generations that have not been born. Gnanakan further posits: "God is the owner of the

29. Presbyterian Eco-Justice Task Force, *Keeping and Healing the Creation*, 37.

30. Ibid., 33.

land (Lev 25) and entrusts to humans the stewardship of keeping and tending it for present future generations. Even the land, not just its produce, being God's creation, has the need to be regenerated, so that it may continue to sustain life."[31] Therefore, awareness is necessary about God's intentions for the earth, which it exists to worship God, to provide for human needs, and to provide for future economic needs of nations. Such an awareness helps a good steward to provide necessary stewardship.

## b) Efforts to Increase and Multiply the Talent

The success of the stewards in the parable of Jesus noticeably was related to their ability to make more talents out of the ones they were given. They traded profitably. Their industry to make profits pleased the master. They were rewarded with eternal rewards for this industry. Successful stewards in environmental stewardship will have the desire and make efforts to increase and multiply whatever resources that are available for them. An exegetical interpretation of the parable of the talents in the book of Luke 19:11–27 reveals the problem why people do not engage in the noble activity of increasing and multiplying the talent. First, there was a problem of people who wanted the kingdom of God but not the King himself. Luke comments that "the people thought that the Kingdom of God was going to appear at once" (Luke 19:11 NIV). But this people, even with their desire for the kingdom to appear at once, did not want the King, and they sent delegation to stop the king from taking over. They sent a delegation after this 'son of noble birth' to say that they did not want that person to be their king. In this parable, the story of people who want the kingdom of God but do not want Jesus to be their Lord is depicted. It is surprising how this part of the scripture is rarely read and understood by the Christians. Christians do not stop to see the relationship Jesus was bringing in saying that there were people who "wanted the kingdom at once," and in sharing his parable of the talents. In essence,

---

31. Gnanakan, *Responsible Stewardship of God's Creation*, 59

## The Position of a Christian as a Steward

Jesus is saying, that some Christian want the kingdom, but do not want to be involved in the kingdom business, because they want the kingdom, but not Jesus, the King. Sometimes this does not become abundantly clear to people. The servants that love the king, will do anything that the king commands, and as a reward, the king will reward them by making them not just citizens in his kingdom, but governors with him.

The second problem why people in this parable did not make profits, was because there were people who wanted the kingdom because of the misconception of rest without toil. These are the people who want the joy and pleasure of reward but are not willing to work for it. Jesus told this story to make it clear that the kingdom of God included working hard to make profit. Those who want the rest must toil, to have something to give, when the Lord comes calling. This worldview is planted by the Devil, accepted by lazy people, and practiced by the evil minded destined to hell. At the end of the story, the lazy steward is thrown outside, where there is crying forever"

The third problem in the minds of the people was some people wanted the kingdom of God 'here and now,' because they did not want to work. These are the people that thought that the Lord was delaying. He was staying too long. These people had a perception that the Lord was wasting time. They were too tired to do anything, they only wanted to enter the rest. Jesus told this story to make it clear that 'work' was part of the kingdom of God, and that rest comes as a reward for those who have done something.

The parable of the talents is the parable of reward and retribution, offered by Jesus the King. These rewards are given to those who had the right mind set of how to wait for the King. These rewards and retribution are based on the work that people do while they wait for the King to come. On the one hand, the people who want the kingdom and the King are completely awake to the reality of coming king. They also remember the instructions given by the Lord, and delight in obeying them. Furthermore, they want to make the most out of the limited time before the return of the king. They did business with the talents, enduring the difficult circumstances of performing a trade. One character of tradesmen is that they have the wisdom to judge the right direction to progress, otherwise the law of the jungle will evict them. Business is about intelligence. About wit. About judgement, and about aggressiveness. It is surprising that this same Jesus who instructed his disciples to be as humble as doves, also prepared them to understand that his kingdom will be about trading with talents, to make profits. Profit requires patience, resistance against the temptation to be ruled by appetites, resilience during hard times and wisdom to understand where one has come from, and the specific strategies employed.

The people who want the kingdom only but not the King are lazily longing for the second coming, meanwhile burdening others. They also remember that there is a kingdom coming, but have forgotten the responsibility and duty of kingdom members. They are so tired of working, that they want the king to come and give them rest. Profit making therefore, is an integral part of the kingdom of God. Unfortunately, many Christians are not aware of this fact, and without their knowledge, fall in one or all of the three wrong worldviews discussed.

Increasing the talents regarding environmental management involves making the available resources to be better, and more valuable. For example, when someone inherits land from their parents, they have the responsibility to improve.

c) Excitement to Account for the Talent

The successful stewards demonstrated great excitement while accounting for the talents they received. The one steward who did not make profit showed his unhappiness with the master giving them assignments and expecting them to account. This was one area in which the stewards were different. Christians are in a position of responsibility too, and their success in environmental stewardship will depend on how they appreciate the act of accountability. God will ask them how they used the environment that was placed under their care.

## The Position of a Christian as a Steward

Accountability is usually a very important element that supports every successful society. Diana Leafe Christian observes that the most common sources of conflict in a community is when some people cannot account for the deeds of commission or omission, preventing other people from effectively executing their parts of the assigned duties.[32] A community that succeeds is the community where members agree, or aware of what is supposed to be done, and are willing to explain the actions and their missed actions. A good steward cheerfully accounts to the community and gets ready to account to the master. Environmental stewardship benefits immensely when members of the community are willing to make rules for each other, or set expectations for each other, and then abide by them, for "the simple desire not to let others down usually becomes an internalized motivator for more responsible behaviour."[33] For example, a community could agree that nobody should dump wastes in the river, or nobody should farm too close to the river. Proper accountability involves members who will not break the rules, because they respect the community, and if they did so, they should be sure that the system expects them to explain why. Accounting system has reinforcements in terms of rewards and punishments. The parable of Jesus puts the reward and punishment at the end. A good community could have these reinforcements spread throughout the time, so that people grow with a desire to account well. Christian posits that "When people repeatedly do not do what they promise, and others continue to hold them accountable, it usually results in the person either changing their habits or eventually leaving the group."[34]

---

32. Christian, "Accountability and Consequences," 16–19.
33. Ibid., 18.
34. Ibid.

CHAPTER THREE

# Environmental Adversity in Kenya
*Opportunity to Change*

A nation that destroys its soils destroys itself. Forests are the lungs of our land, purifying the air and giving fresh strength to our people.

—FRANKLIN D ROOSEVELT

**INTRODUCTION**

KENYA IS ENDOWED WITH immense resources, intelligent people and neighbors with more natural resources to match. The equator divides the country approximately into two halves, and the weather patterns have historically favoured food production. The rivers, lakes, mountains, aquifers, *et cetera* beautify the country even more. The five "water towers" of Kenya –Mount Kenya, the Aberdare Range, the Mau Forest Complex, Mount Eglon, and the Cherangani Hills –are montane forests and the five largest forest blocks in the country. They form the upper catchments of all the main rivers in Kenya (except the Tsavo River originating from Mt Kilimanjaro). The "water towers" are sources of water for irrigation, agriculture, industrial process, as well as to install hydro-power plants, which produce about 60 per cent of Kenya's electricity output.[1] In the recent times however, the climatic changes and environmental degradations have threatened to collapse the entire system. Farmers suffering from unpredictable rainfall patterns and degraded soils have either given up or hope that something would happen, so that they would return to profitability. Water sources have continued to dry or suffer pollution, soil has increasingly become eroded and 'tired,' diseases have increased because of poor environment, and the people have become poorer. While adversity could be something negative, change management practitioners have learned that adversity is usually an opportunity to make a positive transformation in the lives of people. The following section presents environmental adversity in Kenya.

## SYNOPSIS OF ENVIRONMENTAL COLLAPSE IN KENYA

According to Jesse Mugambi the concept of "survival of the fittest" coined by Charles Darwin, which originally was used to apply to animals and plants, is now also a reality for human beings.[2] Kenyans now must grapple with the threat of diminished chances of survival, based on reports of serious degradations. Kenyan environment has in the last three decades witnessed serious ravages according to *The Atlas of our Changing Environment*, and now 80% of Kenya is dry and gradually turning into a desert. Coupled with increased population (in 1960, the Kenyan population was just eight million, poverty, climate change, *et cetera*, Kenya could soon be falling beyond reclamation (Taskforce Report on Forest Resource Management and Logging Activities in Kenya, 2018).[3] The following section provides a quick synopsis of environmental collapse in Kenya.

---

1. United Nations Environmental Program, *Atlas*, 3.
2. Mugambi, *Environment*, i.
3. Thaxton, Integrating Population, Health and Environment, 1.

## a) Food

Agriculture, which is the back bone of the country's economy, offering direct employment to 70% of the population and providing for food, is now threatened. The frequent alternation of drought and floods leads to crop failure. Shortage of freshwater and its poor quality are rampant, significantly limiting development in the country. To make it worse, heavy erosion has depleted the top soil and left bare earth which is not able to sustain crop growth.[4] According to Stephen N Ngigi, Kenya has only about 17% of its total land area available for farming due to rainfall patterns.

The need for food has recently become a pressing concern in Kenya. Kenya's population is increasing by about a million people every year, but the size of the land obviously remains the same. The fact that Kenya is largely arid or semi-arid makes production of food a difficult endeavor.[5] Furthermore, the changing climatic conditions, coupled with decreased land fertility and increased urbanization further compounds the problem in Kenya, worsening the already bad situation. Because of the situation that most of Kenya is, the ability of Kenyans to produce food is severely compromised. The need for innovation and resilience therefore becomes urgent.

Several attempts have been made by various individuals, organizations, and state sectors to respond to the situation. Companies that market seeds have been developing varieties that can withstand adverse conditions, but this has not delivered much results. The government of Kenya has even tried to fund a mega million project in Tana River County to do irrigated farming, similar to what is done in desert countries like Israel. This too has consumed more money than it has produced. Individual farmers have tried creating more land from grassland and forests but the situation is even grimmer. It does not matter that most of what used to be Mau Forest has now been deforested and transformed into crop farms. In 2017, Kenya had to import food from Mexico, a transaction that costed the county a lot of money which could have been used in development and infrastructure.

4. UNDP Website, 2002.
5. UNEP, *Atlas*, 7.

*Environmental Adversity in Kenya*

b) Desertification and Droughts

The meaning of climate change has been the subject of controversy in many countries. According to the United Nations Intergovernmental Panel on Climate Change (IPCC), Climate change refers to a change in the state of the climate identifiable through weather changes that persist for decades. These changes impact the ecosystem, and with agriculture becoming the victim of change, especially because of climate change effects, which usually compromise water and soil potential. A key aspect that is examined in this study relates to desertification and drought. Mark Kipkurwa Boitt and Patrick Ambi Odima concluded that desertification has been sweeping at an alarming rate, with changes becoming evident even in just one decade.[6] The following two photographs show the changes in one decade in one of the counties in Kenyas.

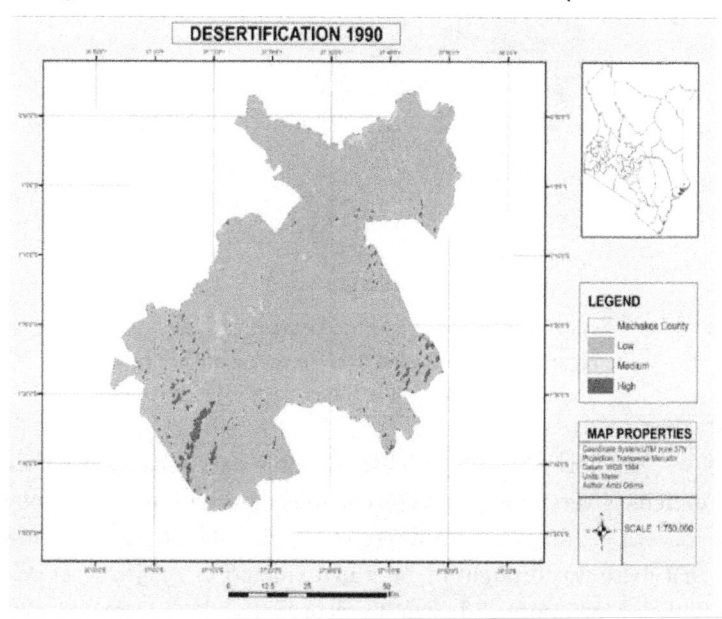

Figure 1: Desertification in Machakos County in 1990 (Boitt and Odima, 2017).

---

6. Boitt & Odima, Desertification Dynamics in Machakos, 40–43.

The figure indicates that the fraction of 'desertified' villages in Machakos County in 1990 compared to the rest of the county was negligible. Although definitions of desertification vary from individual to individual, it is notable that when the same study was done ten years later, desertification was conspicuous, as shown in the figure below.

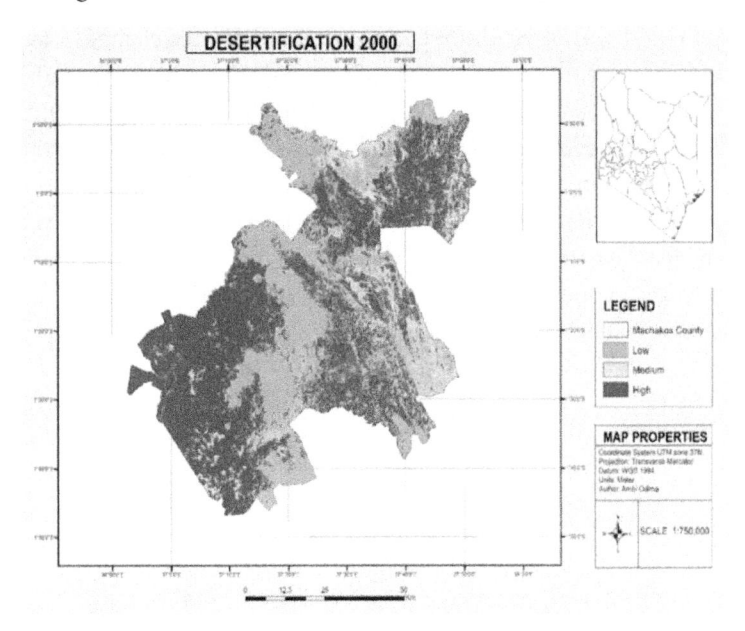

Figure 2: Desertification in Machakos County in 2000
(Boitt and Odima 2017)

The figures show that desertification in Machakos has been extremely very rapid, with conspicuous ramifications. The second concern is drought. According to C. Ackello-Ogutu records show that there was drought in Yatta in 1949 and in 1975–76 period.[7] Tiffen, Mortimore and Gichuki records that there were droughts in 1928–29, 1933–36, 43–46, 1949–1951 and 1975 periods.[8] Other writers Rocheau *et al* record that there was a biting drought

7. Ackello-Ogutu, 'Livestock production,' 89.
8. Tiffen & Gichuki, *More People Less Erosion*, 11.

in 1984–85 period.[9] International Federation of the Red Cross records that Yatta suffered drought in the years: 91/92, 95/96, and 98/2000, with the year 2000 drought being the worst in 37 years.[10] There are thousands of other materials available online that provide discussions related to droughts in Yatta context, which then reveal that this concern is significant. This aggravates the already worse situation of erodible and infertile Yatta soil types: Acrisols, Luvisols, Ferralsols, Alfisols, Ultisols, Oxisols and Lithisols.[11]

The ripple effect of this desert related effect is rise in temperature. According to the UNDP, the mean annual temperature in Kenya has increased by 1.00 C since 1960 representing average rate of 0.21°C per decade. It is projected to increase by 1.0 to 2.8°C by 2060s and by the year 2100, temperatures in Kenya could increase by about 4°C causing variability of rainfall by upto 20 per cent.[12] Given that a large portion of Kenya is semi-arid with high temperatures and low precipitation, frequent droughts, water scarcity, and unpredictable climate variability will have the largest impacts on people living most since it directly or indirectly supports 80% of the population and agro industries support much of Kenya's economy.[13] Kenya's high dependence on natural resources, its poverty levels and how low capacity to adapt, and the existence of other significant environmental stress make it highly vulnerable to the impacts of climate change.[14]

## c) Deforestation

The third concern was wanton deforestation in Kenyan forests. The reality of Kenya's failing environment propelled the government of Kenya in 2018 to set up a task force to review deforestation and

9. Rocheleau, Steinberg, & Benjamin, "Environment, Development, Crisis, and Crusade, 1037.
10. International Federation of the Red Cross, "Kenyan Droughts, 1.
11. Lezberg, "Political ecology and resource management, 1.
12. Kabubo-Mariara, The Economic Impact of Climate Change, 1–38.
13. Ibid.
14. UNEP, *Atlas*, 56.

status of the environment in the country. The task force reported that Kenya's closed canopy forest cover stood at less than 2% of the total land area, compared to the African average of 9.3% and a world average of 21.4 per cent, which means that Kenya is one of the countries with very poor forest cover, even though it is not in the Sahara Desert. The task force also noted that these damaged closed canopy forests were also the source of water in Kenya, and the fact that they were facing extinction means that the future hope of fresh flowing rivers was could slowly be changing into a mirage. The depletion rate, according to this commission was an alarming 5,000 hectares annually.[15]

In the year 2004 Kenya produced her first ever report on the state of its environment mainly focusing on the forest cover. The report documented manifest systematic destruction, with direct relation to population and politics. The country has lost up to "65% of its standing wood volume in just the past 30 years alone."[16] Professor Wangari Maathai is quoted to have said once: "if you destroy the forest then the river will stop flowing, the rains will become irregular, the crops will fail and you will die of hunger and starvation" (Maathai, 2006). The situation in Kenya is that of wanton destruction of existing forest cover. Some of the causal factors are intense population growth around these montane zones between the 1960s and 1990s along with unsustainable exploitation of forest resources, have threatened forest cover. Large areas of indigenous forest have been cleared for tree plantations, extensive illegal logging of valuable species, and small-scale illegal activities such as charcoal production, marijuana growing, and unauthorized farming. Efforts to develop legislations have been futile, as the country lacks good will and mechanism for enforcing those deterring legislation (Atlas of our Changing Environment).

To understand the Kenyan situation, it is best to view this country in the context of the entire continent. According to UNEP report in 2002, "forests cover about 22% of the Africa South of

15. Taskforce to Inquire into Forest Resource Management and Logging Activities, 2018.

16. National Environment Management Authority, 10.

Sahara but are disappearing faster than anywhere else in the developing world. The thickest forest cover for a long time has been the Democratic Republic of Congo. Due to political instability in the country and poor infrastructure, the country's indigenous forest has been the recent target of loggers from all over Africa. It is now common knowledge that the mahogany supply in Nairobi is harvested in Congo. The loss of forest cover began in the 1980s, coinciding with the wake of Africa's post independent political instability. During that decade alone, Africa lost 10.5% of its forest, and the destruction has been relentless."[17] Other research conducted during the following decade of the 1990s demonstrated that Africa lost an estimated 5 million hectares of forest each year.[18] To further elaborate this, Craig Sorley observes that 70% of all Africans rely on wood, charcoal, or plant residues as their primary source of energy, and for many countries, that means that 75–90% or more of all energy consumed comes from wood. As populations grow the number of people depending on these fuels is increasing rapidly.[19]

The foregoing discussion illustrate that destruction of forest cover is a problem witnessed all over Africa. At independence in 1963, the total forest cover was 10% of the country land space area. During the time of the survey in 2003 it was reduced to 1.5%. The rate at which the forest is being destroyed is alarming. The situation is worse now, if a fresh environmental audit is done both in gazetted forests and the so-called community forests, the cover could be below 1%. Records show the glazier in Mount Kenya glazier to have drastically reduced as a result of deforestation.[20] Only 11 of the 18 glaciers that covered Mount Kenya's summit a century ago remain, leaving less than one third of the previous ice cover. The ice on Mount Kenya has also become thinner.[21] The forest cover in Kenya is mostly in Rift Valley highlands and all mountains.

17. UNEP, 2002.
18. Sorley, *Christ and Creation*, 1.
19. Ibid.
20. Hastenrath, *Climate Dynamics of the Tropics*, 3.
21. Ibid.

## Christian Faith and Environmental Stewardship

According to the *Atlas of our Changing Environment*, the Kenyan montane forests are also surrounded by the dense habitations. This is because these areas provide water, fuel wood, construction timber, pasture, and the areas have reliable rainfall throughout the year.[22] The importance of the forest is therefore linked with livelihoods for many Kenyans. Unfortunately, these resources are always harvested in an unsustainable way, due to extensively illegal, irregular, and ill-planned exploitation.

The biggest of the five water towers is the Mau Forest Complex, covering over 400,000 hectares. This is a closed canopy montane forest ecosystem, viewed by many stakeholders as the most important water catchment in the Rift Valley and western Kenya. In addition to deforestation, other human activities contributing to this are land degradation, overgrazing, pollution, loss of biodiversity, and drying rivers.[23] Since the Mau complex is the source of most of the rivers in western Kenya, the livelihoods of the people living in Western, Nyanza, Rift valley regions of Kenya are at stake. Some evidence of this danger is the fact that due to rampart deforestation in the Mau Complex, river Mara dried for the first time in history in 2015. The beautiful scenery of elephants and other animals crossing this river, which usually attract tourists every year, was not there in 2015.

Deforestation means that the Mau Complex, which supports key economic sectors in Kenya including energy, tourism, agriculture, and water supplies for settlement is threatened. The catchment's potential hydropower generation capacity of approximately 535 megawatts, representing about 57% of Kenya's current total electricity generation is also in jeopardy.[24] Tourism which is Kenya's second largest employer and foreign currency earner is at the verge of failure.

The destruction of the Mau Forest Complex has been taking place in the past few decades. In about 35 years, there has been degazettement of forest reserves and continuous widespread

22. Kenya Forest Working Group, 3.
23. Ibid.
24. GoK and UNEP 2008.

encroachment, leading to the destruction of over 100 000 ha of forest since the year 2000. In the last two years of Moi's presidency (2001 and 2002), more than 100,000 hectares were excised including over half of eastern Mau Forest Reserve, damaging permanently the spring and source for Njoro River which drains its eastern slopes into Lake Nakuru, one of Kenya's prime tourist attractions because of flamingo. The other part that was excised is the primary source for River Sondu which is the source of Sondu-Miriu hydropower plant.

One main cause of deforestation is encroachment of human population. The complex is attractive because of reliable rainfall, fertile soil, and the land is free. Furthermore, the communities surrounding the forest, such as the Kisii, the Kipsigis and the Kikuyu have a high rate of population increase rate. Government forest lands are seen as public resources for all to consume. Usually, government enforcement agencies for the protection of forests are limited, and often corrupt. As such, they can only do just so much. In other instances, they feel discouraged, when they protect some parts of the forest only for politicians to use high level corruption to destroy well protected forests, making their efforts seem futile, and making them to be treated with hostility among the local communities.

The second biggest water tower is Mount Kenya. The mountain itself is the highest in the country, and has a great variety of indigenous trees, and still has some attractive snow-caps. The mountain is also tourism scene and has valuable timber. The mountain has forest belt growing between 3,000 and 4,000m, assuring the place of good rainfall that falls throughout the year, making the region a good place for crop farming and animal rearing. This is one reason why there is a growing population living as neighbours of the forest.

This rate of forest loss is unsustainable. The number of trees coming down each year is more than those planted. According to Isaac Kalua of Green Africa Foundation, Kenya is losing 5.6 million trees every day due to charcoal burning, harvesting and collection of firewood. Institutions of learning in Kenya depend on firewood for cooking, raising the demand for fuel wood, and consequently leading to wanton destruction of dwindling forest cover.

The overall impact of forest damage is difficult to calculate. However, there is no doubt about the precarious position Kenyan security and future development is put. For Kenya, a lot of development is geared towards realizing the Vision 2030. Most of the development agencies opine that this vision will be realized only if available natural resources are managed sustainably, especially the five "water towers."

The third biggest water tower is the Aberdare Ranges, covering places around Kenya's capital: Nairobi. The range rises gradually, reaching over 4 000 m at Oldonyo Lesatima, its highest peak. At the west, Aberdare Ranges go as far west as Kijabe and Naivasha, pouring some of its waters to Lakes Naivasha and Elementaita in the Rift Valley. The Eastern borders are the slopes that gradually, carry water into the Tana River (where the Seven Forks hydropower plants is built, and where over half of Kenya's electricity is generated). Some of the tributaries feeding River Tana are Rivers Chania and Thika, which also feed two important dams: Sasumua and Ndakaini. These dams are the main sources of water for Nairobi City's more than three million people. The Aberdare's also form part of the upper catchments of the Athi, Ewaso Nyiro, and Malewa Rivers.

Out of the entire range, the forest alone covers over 250 000 hectares. This forest benefits from the protection of the gazetted protected forest such as the escarpments of the Aberdare, Kikuyu Escarpment, Kijabe Hill, Kipipiri, and Nyamweru which have endangered species such as African Red Cedar. Furthermore, the Aberdare National Park which covers 760 km2 adds to the protection of this water tower. The range is characterized by a high diversity of tree and forest types due to the wide altitudinal range (1 800 to 3 600 meters) and climatic differences between slopes, making it the most diverse forest cover in Kenya.

Despite the foregoing benefits, large-scale, uncontrolled, irregularly, or illegal human activities, charcoal production, logging, encroachment and settlements, cultivation of marijuana and other crops, and livestock grazing are devastating the Aberdare Ranges. This particular water has also proved to be very difficult to secure, since it is surrounded by aggressive inhabitants, and construction demands in Nairobi. Communities living around the Aberdare have had historical cultures of residing in the forest, which was successful in the colonial war, but did not stop after independence. As such, the government enforcement officers are usually unable to protect the forest from illegal loggers. Protected Kijabe strip for example, which has high quality red cedars, have been destroyed consistently, by illegal loggers who have proved too difficult to eradicate. The onslaught on these forests has already led to drying of certain streams and rivers. In the Kijabe strip alone, there used to be four streams that flowed continuously as recent as 1990. However, with the systematic destruction of the protected Kijabe strip, three out of the four streams have dried. In fact, the one stream feeding Kijabe hospital is still flowing from the remaining forest cover protected by the Church. Recently, the hospital has had to engage in an expensive exercise of getting piped water from Bathi Dam in Kimende, because the one river supplying their water is no longer enough.

Mount Elgon is another strong water tower, which for a long time remained un-tampered. Like the Aberdare Ranges, forest cover at Mount Elgon benefits from the protection Mount Elgon National Park, Chepkitale National Reserve, and Mt Elgon Forest Reserve (which covers 73 706 hectares). Two major rivers, Nzoia and Turkwel, and several streams have their sources in Mount Elgon. These water bodies provide water for dense communities living in Kenya and Uganda. According to the Atlas of our Changing Environment, Mount Elgon forest contains globally threatened species, including some, endemic to the Afro-montane region and others endemic to Mount Elgon alone, making the area a priority for species conservation and a major attraction for tourists.[25]

Mount Elgon faces challenges like Aberdare Ranges, where more than two million people living and depending on the forest are exerting insurmountable pressure on this unique ecosystem.

25. UNEP, *Atlas of our Changing Environment*, 2009.

Authorized logging has been practiced in Mt Elgon since at least the 1930s. In the 1970s, land was excised from the Mt Elgon Forest around Chebyuk where 600 families were settled to make way for a national game reserve. While a 1986 Presidential Decree banned all logging in Kenya's natural forests, it excluded Mt Elgon where legal logging continues. This means that Mount Elgon was left exposed more than any other forest. In addition to the authorized loggers, agricultural encroachment and charcoal production have added to the ure of forest degradation. The type of agriculture practiced is unsustainable, usually leading to erosion and landslides, and consequently resulting in dam siltation.

The Sabaot Land Defence Forces' war that started in early 2000s, with one clan fighting with another, led not just to the death of human being, but to insurmountable destruction of the forest cover in Mount Elgon. This single incidence that protracted over a period of about five years, resulted in the greatest destruction of forest than any other incidence in the history of Mount Elgon. The fighting warriors used the forest both as military hideout and as a fighting field, targeting people of opposing clans. When the government posted the Kenya Defence Forces to combat the local fighting forces, they also used the forest as hideout and fighting zone, targeting Sabaot Land Defence Forces. Over and over again, the different forces in the forest would fell trees, set fire in the forest to get rid of the 'enemies,' cook using wood in the forest, and often sell trees to neighbouring communities through corrupt means, in order to raise money for surviving in war. The need to enforce forest laws had been overtaken by a more urgent need of controlling the inter-clan fighting.

The smallest of the five water towers in Kenya is the Cherangani Hills. This natural resource, at the Elgeiyo Marakwet, West Pokot and Trans Nzoia Counties is a series of gently rolling hills, rising to 3365m above sea level, that form an undulating upland plateau, partially due to the process of its formation. Cherangany Hills were formed as non-volcanic fault-block. The tree cover at Cherangany is largely the gazetted protected indigenous forest reserves. Cherangany Hills is the source of big rivers such as the

Nzoia River. The recent encroachment from all sides has threatened the forest cover in a way never witnessed before in history. The encroachment is not just because of population alone, but also because of the agricultural demands for new land to satisfy the food market in the country, especially in Baringo and West Pokot counties. Another factor at play was the enthnic competition, especially with the arrival of the Kisii, and Kikuyu who encroached from Kitale, adding ure to the forest land, effectively catalyzing deforestation.

In 2003, a joint project of UNEP and the Department of Resource Survey and Remote Sensing reported that the Cherangani Hills was the least destroyed (comparing with the other four major water towers). There was only a piece of land approximately 174 hectares that had been destroyed. In the following decade however, accelerated forest destruction was witnessed, such that the Embobut forest for instance had been destroyed by April 2013. Human population was not just doing farming in the protected forest land, but also settlements had been established. Cherangany Hills became the target of cedar loggers, from as far as Nairobi. The enforcement officers along the roads periodically arrested trucks ferrying cedar posts, but instead of arrests being deterrents, they became lucrative business for the corrupt police officers.

The disturbance of Cherangani Hills forest also meant that the opportunities offered by the forest were also disturbed. For example, according to the *Atlas of Our Changing Environment*, the Cherangany Hills bear scenic features suitable for ecotourism and are home to the rare De Brazza's Monkey, almost endemic to this forest. Further, the Hills are also classified as an important Bird Area (IBA) in Kenya, attracting more than 73 different forest-dependent species, making the forest one of the leading bird tourist attraction site, second to Arabuko Sokoke forest in Malindi. Out of these bird species, four are regionally threatened, which means that Cherangany Hills offered the best opportunity for protecting these birds. According to Nyagito, developing countries such as Kenya should be the last to waste their tourist opportunities, because of the potential of the revenues collected from tourism, and even those from export of raw natural resources, flowers and agricultural commodities.[26] Even with the demand for food alone, the Kenya community need to put into considerations the fact that many poor households depend on environment available to them for growing their own food. For a community to be regarded as food secure, the production of food should be secure, affordable, and predictable. This is not guaranteed however, in places like the Cherangany Hills where the encroachment and destruction is wanton. Poor soils and low agricultural productivity, lack of control over land management, and competition from other users are some of the conditions that threaten household food security.[27]

The situation in Cherangany is particularly grave, bearing in mind that over 36% of all the rural poor Kenyans live on marginal lands or areas that are particularly vulnerable to environment degradation, such as floodplains, coastal areas, and degraded hillsides. Depending on such lands for food can render poor people vulnerable to periodic hunger. Environmental hazards and extreme events, such as droughts, floods, forest fires, and landslides, are more damaging in marginal and degraded ecosystems and the poor living there are least able to cope with their impacts. For all these reasons, achieving the first MDG –eradicating extreme poverty and hunger –requires renewed efforts towards achieving MDG 7, through the sustainable management of land, water, biodiversity resources, and the adequate provision of urban sanitation, potable water, and waste management.[28]

The dominant vegetation in Yatta constituency is dry bush.[29] The problem was further compounded by laxity or unwillingness of farmers to plant trees.[30] According to Munyao, Muisu, Mbengo, Mburu, and Sirma:

26. Nyagito & Okello, Kenya's agricultural policy and sector performance, 1.

27. UNEP, *Atlas*, 55.

28. Ibid.

29. Lezberg, "Political ecology and resource management, 1.

30. Munyao, Muisu, Mbego, Mburu, & Sirma, "Influence of Land Size on Jatropha, 42.

> Despite the potentially important role Jatropha can play in Yatta District and notwithstanding the many agencies such as NGOs, private investors and churches involved in the promotion of *Jatropha curcas* cultivation in the country, its uptake remains low. This may perhaps because of unavailability of land for *Jatropha curcas* cultivation.[31]

Although these authors' interest was only on the cultivation of Jatropha curcas, it is notably interesting that the people of Yatta did not plant other types of trees, even those which the local people thought to be directly beneficial in the providence of fruits. Many farmers are reported to have preferred crop farming and livestock herding over planting of trees (Ibid). An article by Benson Kamau Mburu, James Biu Kung'u, and Njagi Muriuki (2015) point out to the fact that a lot of deforestation happening in Yatta is for charcoal burning. They observe:

> The farmers pointed out that they use species such as *Terminaliabrownii* (Fresen), Dalbergiamelanoxylon (Guill.&Perr), *Acacia tortilis* (Forssk.), *Acacia senegal* (L.) Willd, *Melia volkensii*, *Albiziaanthelmintica* (Brongn) and*Acacia mellifera* (Vahl) *Benth* among others for charcoal making. All these are trees of significant ecological importance in the dry lands. From field observations and farmers' responses regarding species that used to be common in Yatta area but are now very difficult to find, it was evident that charcoal burning has contributed to the disappearance of some of these species. Species such as *Dalbergiamelanoxylon* and *Albiziaanthelmintica* are quite rare in Yatta district. Indeed, *Dalbergiamelanoxylon* is listed in the IUCN Red List (2010) as a near threatened species.[32]

---

31. Ibid.

32. Mburu, Kung'u, & Muriuki, "Climate change adaptation strategies, 716.

### d) Water Scarcity

A friend once shared a story about a particular question that appeared in national primary examination in late 1970s: what is the color of water? He noted that during his time, because of the clear rivers, and the fertile black soil, he thought the water was black. About 30 years later, one of his sons was writing is primary certificate exam. He asked him that same question; the boy answered that the color of water was brown. This illustrates how the water in the country has not only changed in quality, but reduced in quantity.

As noted earlier, most of the country is arid or semi arid. Twenty percent of the country receives regular rainfall. The rest receive less rain usually not more than 700 mm annually, and which would not support crop farming.[33] A book by Hezron Mogaka, Samuel Gichere, Richard Davis and Rafik Hirji (2005) reports that water scarcity due to droughts, or water degradation to floods cost Kenya about 16 billion shillings every year, equivalent to 2.4% of the GDP, which is a serious encumbrance to the country's economy.[34] Titus Masika (2016) points out that water scarcity was a major struggle for the people of Yatta Plateau, and one of the main reason why he sprang up to action when he heard that people were dying in Yatta due to lack of drinking water and food.

### e) Degradation of Pasturelands

The fifth concern was overgrazing. A relevant article that follows this problem historically was Peberdy (1958). He noted that the first government-posted District Agricultural Officer to Machakos in 1931, Mr Leckie, sought to work with Local Native Council (LNC) to rehabilitate an 80-hectare steep, badly eroded land. He intended to use this as a case that would serve as a demonstration for future endeavors. He employed methods such as planting of Mauritius

---

33. Ngigi, *Review of Irrigation Development in Kenya*, 3.

34. Mogaka, Gichere, Davis, & Hirji, "Climate Variability and Water Resources Degradation in Kenya, 7.

beans along the trench banks, keeping off the cattle, planting exotic drought resistant forage plants, supplying gullies with wash stops *et cetera*. A nursery was set up to supply fodder plants, trees, and wash-stop grasses, such as the Mexican daisy, spineless cactus, Napier, woolly-finger, Bermuda and crested wheat grass, Kudzu vine, black Mauritius bean, and drought-resistant fodder trees and shrubs.[35] Furthermore, persuasion by the government administrators improved the adoption rate. These efforts were complemented by a regular supply of prisoners' labor for reconditioning work; introduction of meat factory to easy the culling of cattle and persuaded the Akamba to use the money gained from sale of their cattle to buy carts necessary for the transport of manure.[36] Even with such efforts that seem relevant, the move was vehemently resisted, because it was being enforced by a government administrator. The demand for pasture and poor government intervention meant that it became difficult to control pasture in Yatta, and this contributed to environmental collapse.

According to Holling "resilience determines the persistence of relationships within a system and is a measure of the ability of these systems to absorb change of state variable, driving variables, and parameters, and still persist."[37] As Holling further observe, resilience is a component of the system which determines whether the system will persist in certain circumstances, or it will become extinct. In this study, examination of CIM's environmental management activities related to building resilience, will focus on aspects in which Yatta society has been transformed to persist.

## CONCLUSION

The downward trajectory that has been witnessed in several Kenyan zones show that interventions have become necessary. In history, changes that happen in large scale require institutions of

---

35. Kenya Department of Agriculture, 1932.
36. Ibid.
37. Holling, Resilience and Stability of Ecological Systems, 17.

influence, and leadership that is deliberate, committed and willing to pay the price. The Kenyan situation discussed above is not a temporal problem. It is a problem of all time and requires a solution of all times. Unless a deliberate, well concerted mechanism is put in place as an intervention, unsustainable practices in the community are likely to continue unabated for a long time. This should be done in cognizance of the fact that when communities do not receive proper guidance and mentorship on what options to choose from, they are likely, in their despair to make detrimental decisions that would harm the very systems that support them. Drought and desertification have become increasingly recurring in Kenya, a factor which led to the people to desire urgent interventions.

CHAPTER FOUR

# Christian Worldview of Environmental Stewardship

So the final conclusion would surely be that whereas other civilizations have been brought down by attacks of barbarians from without, ours had the unique distinction of training its own destroyers at its own educational institutions, and then providing them with facilities for propagating their destructive ideology far and wide, all at the public expense. Thus did Western Man decide to abolish himself, creating his own boredom out of his own affluence, his own vulnerability out of his own strength, his own impotence out of his own erotomania, himself blowing the trumpet that brought the walls of his own city tumbling down, and having convinced himself that he was too numerous, labored with pill and scalpel and syringe to make himself fewer. Until at last, having educated himself into imbecility, and polluted and drugged himself into stupefaction, he keeled over—a weary, battered old brontosaurus—and became extinct.

—MALCOLM MUGGERIDGE, VINTAGE MUGGERIDGE: RELIGION AND SOCIETY

# Christian Faith and Environmental Stewardship

## INTRODUCTION

THE COMPLETE CHRISTIAN DICTIONARY for home, school and office, (2002) defines worldview as the way in which a matter is judged, so that the background, future or possible problems are taken into consideration. This definition assumes that worldview comes into play only when judgement of a matter is required. Del Tacket introduces an aspect of "making sense of life." He defines worldview as "the framework from which we view reality and make sense of life and the world."[1] In other words, worldview has to do with how a person views and interprets what is happening in the world around him/her. Worldview therefore is our perspective of how we see things. This brings to the fore the fact that our response to different issues and things in life sometimes differs from the responses of others.

Worldview is a powerful instrument that motivates people to certain actions. It is worldview that drives suicide bombers to perform their wicked acts. Their mind-sets are tuned to see success and a sense of accomplishment in killing certain groups of people. It is worldview that makes certain heads of state to resign from power after failing to marshal requisite support for certain bills in parliament, while other heads of state cling to power even after they become unpopular. It is this worldview that makes certain churches to cut down trees to create space for parking vehicles, while other churches plant trees so that their members may understand how the earth looked like, when God saw that "it was good."

In relation to environmental management, it is good to note that environmental stewardship success depends on how people view nature. When they have a positive view of it, they are likely to appreciate its contribution, as well as exert valued time and resources to see it flourish. Worldviews related to environmental stewardship could be supportive or destructive. Many people that hold supportive views, do so because they understand the environment either to be a refuge and source of benefits for humanity, or that it has some intrinsic value in itself. The view that the earth has

1. Tacket, "What's a Christian Worldview?" 1.

intrinsic value helps to show that God did not put human beings as the only center of creation, because even without humans, the biosphere has "a value in itself"[2] (Rolston 2006, 307). Following this therefore, it can be argued that humans have a duty to preserve the integrity of the environment, for its own advantage, to exercise what its designer wanted to achieve. Such supportive worldviews influence people to care for the environment. Destructive worldviews however, exist. These worldviews propel people to act in such a way that the environment is degraded. Sometime, people do not know or agree that they hold those views, but their actions towards environment reveal the kind of mind-set they have. The following section presents some existing negative worldviews, which do not help in environmental stewardship.

## DESTRUCTIVE WORLDVIEWS ON ENVIRONMENT

## a) All things on Earth were created for Human Enjoyment

The first potential worldview which inhibit environmental stewardship is the view that the things on earth were created for the very purpose of human enjoyment. According to John Calvin, "the end for which all things were created [was] that none of the convenience and necessities of life might be wanting to men."[3] This view that humanity is the center of creation, and that God had Adam in focus when he was creating everything, a view widely held by many people, do not come out of the Bible after all. A passage usually used to support this view of humans being at the center is Genesis 1:26–28. The Barnes notes on Genesis 1:28 notes that:

> Power is presumed to belong to man's nature, according to the counsel of the Maker's will in Genesis 1:26. But without a special permission he cannot exercise any lawful authority. For the other creatures are as independent of him as he is of them. As creatures he and they are on an equal footing and have no natural fight either over the

2. Rolston, III., "Caring for Nature," 307.
3. Calvin, Institutes of Christian Religion, 22.

> other. Hence, it is necessary that he should receive from high heaven a formal charter of right over the things that were made for man. He is therefore authorized, by the word of the Creator, to exercise his power in subduing the earth and ruling over the animal kingdom. This is the meet sequel of his being created in the image of God. Being formed for dominion, the earth and its various products and inhabitants are assigned to him for the display of his powers.[4]

This commentary of Genesis 1:28 discusses the conclusion that emerge out of exegesis of this text, which as noted, points out to the fact Adam was given some form of supervisory roles over the other creation. The creation then is to meet human needs. Barnes further points out that this God's intention was not for Adam benefit selfishly, but to be a leader that ensures benefits for the entire creation, as seen in this quote:

> The subduing and ruling refer not to the mere supply of his natural needs, for which provision is made in the following verse, but to the accomplishment of his various purposes of science and beneficence, whether towards the inferior animals or his own race. It is the part of intellectual and moral reason to employ power for the ends of general no less than personal good. The sway of man ought to be beneficent.[5]

This exegesis by Barnes, that God's intention for the rule of Adam was for everything in the creation to benefit, truly conveys God's purposes and is consistent with the entire scripture. A superficial reading of Genesis 1:26–28 has led several people to make unwarranted conclusion that man is the center of universe, and that everything was created for him, a view which I regard as anthropocentrism. In this matter, Hillary Marlow observes that the view of humans being the center affects profoundly human treatment of the environment, as noted here:

---

4. Barnes, "Barnes Notes on the Bible," 1.
5. Ibid.

Such a human-centered perspective on God's world seems to take little account of the diversity, complexity and, to our minds, strangeness of much of the natural world, which is now accessible to us through a wealth of nature films and documentaries. But it also carries a more profound theological weakness affecting our view of God as well as of the world and can lead us to a self-centered and childish understanding of God as the one who always gives us whatever we want. If we see the rest of the world- the 'non-human creation'- as existing purely for human benefit, we fail to take seriously either the creation or its creator. Such attitudes have contributed to exploitative and damaging practice in many parts of the world, as human beings have tried to take what they regarded as their right, without regard for the consequences.[6]

Anthropocentricism is therefore a view that is totally against the Biblical teaching. This could be why Lynn White Junior, in his article "The Historical Roots of Our Ecologic Crisis" blamed Christianity for environmental irresponsibility.[7] According to White, Christian perspective of dominion gives them unsanctioned freedom to exploit whatever resource is available. The problem of the perspective given by White is called 'dominion.' It is a perspective where a human being is taking the center stage of all that was created. The assumed idea is that nature was created for no other purpose, save to serve man. White even goes one step further stating that Genesis (Gen 1:26–28) makes it God's will that man executes his dominion over the natural environment, concluding in his article that regarding our current environmental decay "Christianity bears a huge burden of guilt."[8]

Passmore also provides another perspective from Genesis 1:28, which says: "And God blessed them, and God said unto them, Be fruitful, and multiply, and replenish the earth, and subdue it: and have dominion over the fish of the sea, and over the fowl of the

---

6. Marlow, *The Earth is the Lord's*, 5.
7. White, "The Historical Roots of Our Ecologic Crisis," 1203.
8. White, Jr., "The Historical Roots of Our Ecologic Crisis," 1206.

air, and over every living thing that moved upon the earth" (1:28). According to Passmore, this specific statement on the relationship between man and nature could easily give rise to a radical interpretation of Christianity's reading on creation, in which man is entitled to rule over nature with whatever means available.[9]

Both White and Passmore argued that the dominant interpretation of the Christian doctrine produced a dominion or "man-over-nature" orientation, with which the state of the environment does not concern Christians. Although the dominion theory is not evident in day to day Christian activities, the dominion attitude is prevalent amongst many of them. Many Christians do not show concern to care for the environment. Research has shown that in some instances, wherever some Christian movements swept, in addition to faith, education, and industrialization, environmental degradation also followed.

According to Edward Brown, "dominion" as used in Gen 1:26–28, ought to mean ruler-ship for leading a harmony of all that was created, like a choir conductor. Brown says, "Yes God has made us leaders and rulers. . . to lead the cosmic choir in which worship of the creator is performed." The choir leader, Brown asserts, need to be questioned if the worship is not beautiful, harmonious, *et cetera*. If the choir is dying, the leader is even called to account. The leader needs to be a responsible choir master. He needs to encourage the faint. He needs to support the weak, not to plunder nor destroy. The objective of the choir is not to please the choir leader. The case in the world now, as Brown puts it, is the case where some species are going extinct. Definitely something will go missing when there are no more lions or elephants, or rhinos. Definitely something is wrong, now that millions of species are extinct already. Brown asks "what kind of choirmasters are we, when the choir is being destroyed under our own hands?"[10]

Professor Calvin DeWitt deals with the question of dominion from the perspective of the meaning of the Hebrew words *radah* and *kabash*, which have been translated "have dominion/

9. Passmore, *Man's Responsibility for Nature*, 7.
10. Brown, *Our Father's World*, 39–40.

rule" and "subdue" respectively. In order to apply well the requirements of the commands (to rule/have dominion, and to subdue) it is important to understand the meaning of the words in the context in which they were given. It is also important to see how the word is used elsewhere, in order to properly understand the usage of the word. Radar is used Deuteronomy 17:18-20 as requirements for the kings, that those to whom God gives dominion must fully reflect God's will in their rule.[11] The word is also used in Ezekiel 34:2-4 where the king is being blamed that "you have ruled (*radah*) them harshly. . ."[12] God shows the right kind of *radah* in Ezekiel 34:11, 13, 15-16).[13] In brief, the meaning of *radah* is ruler-ship that develops, rather than domination that degrade. It is committing self to serve others rather than using others to serve self. A similar word is used about Jesus who offers himself to redeem many. Lest people take mandate to subdue the earth as a license to serve self rather than God and creation, God judges between those who use creation with care, and those who abuse it. Those who use their rule to degrade, God says, "is it not enough for you. . . must you trample. . ."[14] Dominion then is best understood in terms of reflecting God's love for the world, God's law for creation, and God's justice for the land and creatures.[15] Without the example of Jesus Christ, DeWitt asserts, one might conclude that this passage suggests "anything goes." However, Jesus Christ brings us to see this dominion as service rather than as license for ungodly behavior.[16] In scriptural language, domination, defined as seeking first ourselves at the expense of creation, is "missing the mark," it's failing to meet the Creator's expectation of us, it is sin.[17]

11. DeWitt, *Caring for Creation*, 42.
12. Ibid.
13. Ibid.
14. DeWitt, *Caring for Creation: Responsible Stewardship of God's Handiwork*, 42
15. Ibid., 42.
16. Ibid., 41.
17. Ibid., 44.

Hillary Marlow describes the meaning of "to have dominion and subdue' in the understanding of the Old Testament people. According to these cultures, the responsibility of a king was to rule well over both people and land, and to represent the god to the people. This picture of kingship is clearly exed in Psalm 72, which links together the king as guarantor of justice and righteousness in society with the wellbeing and fertility of the land. According to Marlow, it is this model of benevolent leadership that is behind Genesis 1:26–27, and which continues in verse 28 using the language of ruling, as human beings are told that they will subdue and have dominion over other animals. But these words form part of a divine blessing, rather than as many interpreters assume, a set of commands. God's injunction to 'be fruitful and multiply and fill the earth' in verse 28, is the same as that given to the fish and birds on day five of creation (verse 22) and is an exion of his desire for the flourishing and fecundity of the creatures he has made. This is echoed in verses 29–30 which details God's provision of food for humans and animals alike.

Therefore, dominion does not mean using the natural resources with supping power. It is stewardship. Abusing resources is what Dewitt calls domination. He says, dominion as domination is forbidden. The right Dominion as stewardship is required as a God-given responsibility for all people. Human dominion, however, is exercised across a broad spectrum, one end of which is dominion exercised in behalf of self and the other dominion in behalf of creation. Dominion at the first extreme can be called domination; dominion at the other extreme can be called stewardship. More specifically, in relation to creation, domination is service to creation in behalf of the Creator. Thus, we can distinguish between two kinds of dominion: domination and stewardship.[18]

Another perspective of understanding dominion is what has been given by Nola Stewart.[19] According to Stewart, the Hebrew verb we translate as 'rule', *'radah'* derives from a noun RADA,

18. DeWitt, *Caring for Creation: Responsible Stewardship of God's Handiwork*, 43.

19. Stewart, *Caring for Creation*, 2.

meaning 'a point higher up on the root of a plant.'[20] It's the place at the top of the root from which shoots radiate above ground and roots radiate below the soil. It is also the center of strength for the plant. Stewart therefore avers that the verb '*radah*' is forceful and defines our ecological role in relation to nature—we are to be the center of strength for all living things in the biosphere. According to her, there is no sense of ownership in '*rada*' nor of unrestricted use.

We must be clear, therefore, about what dominion does and does not mean. While all things have been subordinated to human beings, we should rule over them as God himself does. This dominion does not grant to us the right to "lord over" creation in a manner incongruous with God's own manner of governance. Since the first moment of creation, God has provided for the needs of his creatures, and, likewise, has ordered all of creation to its perfection. Hence man's dominion over creation must serve the good of human beings and all of creation as well. Thus dominion requires responsible stewardship. . . if man exercises dominion in a way that ultimately destroys nature's creative potential or denies the human family the fruits of creation, such action constitutes an offence against God's original plan for creation.[21]

Another key word used in Hebrew is *shamar*, which is translated 'keep.' Adam is given the instruction to *shamar* the garden. Gen 2:15. . . here we learn that Adam and his descendants are expected to serve and keep the garden. The proper meaning of the word *shamar* is clear in the context of the Aaronic blessing given in Numbers 6:24. In this context, the blessing spoken is for God to *shamar* (keep) them in all their vitality, with energy and beauty.[22] To *shamar* the environment therefore, is to ensure it remains with all its vitality, energy and beauty. In addition to recognizing the fullness of the meaning of *shamar* in Genesis 2:15, it is also helpful to our understanding of stewardship to attend to the preceding

20. Ibid., 30.

21. Acton Institute, *Environmental Stewardship*, 39.

22. DeWitt, *Caring for Creation: Responsible Stewardship of God's Handiwork*, 44

word, *abad*... to serve... also in Joshua 24:15.[23] Marlow opines that *abad* can be translated to serve and to preserve. The depiction of Eden in these verses might draw on the tradition of Mesopotamian kings for cultivating royal parks, which is known to us from ancient carvings. If so, the first human is not just any old gardener, he is the royal gardener, answerable to the king himself, that is, to the Lord God (see v 16). Although the imagery is different from the first creation account, the common theme of kingship binds these two chapters together. In Genesis 1 our responsibility as, human beings toward the rest of creation comes to the fore in the idea of servant kingship, ruling wisely and well over God's world. Here in Genesis 2 it is the role of human beings as servants of the one great king, God, which is stressed, with our responsibility before God for tending his garden, the earth, as an act of service and indeed worship towards him.

The Biblical expectation that human beings will "serve the garden" means that our dressing, tilling, and tending are done as acts of service. With the prefix con, this can be applied to indicate "service with," as with the word con-serve.[24] The key to proper service always is to consider our service as Christ's service. Our service should reflect God's love for the world.[25]

Question on whether Christianity univocally lead to less environmental concern are there. There are arguments showing that the sweep of Christianity, instead of being followed by environmental devastation, was a "greening" influence.[26] There is evidence of different Christian denominations that have supported environmental management. Contrary to dominion, the stewardship perception of the man-nature relationship states that the taking care of nature is a clear task that God has assigned to humanity. This worldview has the potency to lead individual Christians to be more concerned about the environment.

23. Ibid., 45.

24. DeWitt, *Caring for Creation: Responsible Stewardship of God's Handiwork*, 45.

25. Ibid., 46.

26. Nash, *The Rights of Nature*, 44.

## Christian Worldview of Environmental Stewardship

Today our planet faces an environmental crisis wrought by the ever-increasing demands and changes of its human population. Ironically it is this same humanity which God designated to care for the earth, not to destroy it. Yet humans have become a modern-day example of a fox...put in charge of the hen house. Our interests have been self-centred.[27] John Calvin presents an ideal situation:

> The custody of the garden was given to Adam, to show that we possess the things which God has committed to our hands, on the condition, that being content with the frugal and moderate use of them, we should take care of what shall remain. Let him who possesses a field, so partake of its yearly fruits, that he may not suffer the ground to be injured by negligence; but let him endeavor to hand it down to posterity as he received it, or even better cultivated. Let him so feed on its fruits, that he neither dissipates it by luxury, nor permits it to be marred or ruined by neglect... Let everyone regard himself as the steward of God in all things which he possesses.[28]

Paul clearly indicates that everything was created by Christ and for Christ as God (Col 1:15). Anthropocentricism, as Attfield puts it, "denies that nature is sacred, belief in the rights of animals is rejected, the value of science and technology is reaffirmed, and the preservation of human civilization is presented as the central morality."[29]

Millard Erickson asserts that proper definition of the term "*adam*" (which was also given as a name for the first male human being), reveals that God had the entire humanity in mind, when he provided natural resources for his consumption and enjoyment. Erickson observes that Adam was a definite historical individual, but nevertheless, he and his wife Eve were the entire human race at that point. Adam contained within him, germinally or seminally, all humans who ever will be within the span of history. God did

---

27. Dyke, Mahan, Sheldon, & Brand, *Redeeming Creation*, 14.
28. Calvin, in Sorley, *Christ and Creation*, 63.
29. Attfield, *The Ethics of Environmental Concern*, 371

not promise and provide to Adam alone the rest of creation as a benefit for humans. God did not intend for Adam alone to enjoy its benefits. God intended for all the benefits to accrue to all members of humanity; always.[30]

## b) Environment is Secular

There is another worldview that environmental management is secular and joining hands with non-Christian environmentalist is forming unholy alliances. According to this view, such endeavors are prohibited by Paul in 2 Corinthians 6:14. This further leads to compartmentalization of what is holy and what is profane, defining environmental management as the later. A careful examination of the exhortation by Paul, not to be yoked together with unbelievers, shows that, the context was about idol worship, and that believers needed to break all connections with idol worshippers irrespective of their familial relationship. Using this passage to keep Christians from uniting with their non-Christian counterparts, means that, environment itself is being removed and separated from God, as something different, an object of worship. In as much as some extremists worship the environment, many Christian environmental stewards care for the environment as a way of worshipping the creator God. Environmental management is not the end in itself.

## c) Environmental Stewardship require a lot of funds

Closely related to a worldview discussed above, is another defeatist approach that depends on overseas funding for environmental management to take place. People with this mind-set have grown or have been brought up in situations negatively affected by donor funding. Bishop Titus Masika avers:

> Africa's problems amount to much more than the trillions of dollars, pumped into the continent as foreign aid, can solve. It is believed that in the last fifty years, Africa has

---

30. Erickson in Land, & Moore, *The Earth Is the Lord's*, 8.

received several trillion dollars in aid, yet there is little to show for it. These funds have gone into oiling corruption and undertaking facility-based development that has not led to expected human development.[31]

Environmental management done by "redeemed people of God" ought to be done out of reverence and worship to the creator, not out of abundance of donor funding. Most of these donor funding usually is meant for those organizations that purport to do development. According to Masika, some international organizations "spend 60 out of every 100 dollars purely on internal costs and only deliver 40 dollars to the community."[32] This explains why organizations spend a lot of money and time and have nothing to show in the long run. These organizations usually find few success stories and use these testimonies as though there was only one factor that led to their successes. Some of the testimonies used for raising money are rehearsed for recording purposes, after which are used all over the world for fund raising, sometimes without the knowledge of those people. In fact, the owners of those NGOs are entrepreneurs who do their selfish fundraising in the name of mission. Their organizations are only conduits of freebies.

Environmental management, like any development activity, need to be done by people who have internal conviction and drive. Non-Governmental Organizations only come in as catalysts, not the drivers. Even with the presence of these expatriates, focus should be the engagements of local people and grass root structures. Most of the expatriates understand only one way of community development: pulling some people out of the village, taking them to an expensive hotel, spend all the money paying for their accommodation, and giving them lectures organized in power point slides. At the end of the workshops, they are given one minute each to say something, with the hope that they will say the conference had really changed them. Usually these expatriates are eager to record those statements, to show their funding organizations that they are doing "work." Most of these expatriates

31. Masika, Mindset Change, 29–30.
32. Masika, *Mindset Change*, 91.

do not have practical experience of what they are talking about. They only read books, or plagiarize power point slides, but on the ground cannot tell the difference between a black jack and a bean. What is lacking is what is termed by Masika as "incarnational encounters with the community."[33] The planning, rehearsing, slides, questions, answers and even conclusions are pre-arranged in an office, to be presented in the hotel. The end of one conference is usually followed by the planning of another, without careful evaluation of what was achieved, and whether communities are being developed. These organizations usually take pride at how many people they have trained, and their key word is 'capacity building.'

Individual contribution matter in environmental stewardship. A story is told of a missionary in Garissa, Kenya, who had a discussion with some idle men he found in town. The missionary was wondering why the men were idle, yet it had been raining very well in the previous weeks. He was expecting that this community, which rarely receives good rainfall, would take advantage of the fortune and plant seeds, to produce their own food. Apparently, this community had entered a government relief program, receiving free food every month. The young idle men told the missionary that they would prefer to wait for a relief truck that was expected in two weeks, rather than plant seeds that would take at least three months before they were harvested. The supply of relief food in Kenya has been going on for decades, and in more than half of the counties in the whole country. According to Titus Masika, relief food, commonly called *mwolyo* in Kikamba language, is one single factor that has ironically promoted poverty. The World Food Policy 2012 report indicates that 66% of funds were spent in Africa, dealing majorly with relief food. Masika asks:

> How could a continent blessed with vast resources such as gold, diamond, copper, iron ore, cobalt, oil, natural gas, titanium, uranium, wildlife, rivers, lakes, mountains, and forests, and people turn out to be a net recipient of

---

33. Masika, *Mindset Change*, 91.

donation from the West? What has gone wrong with and what continues to feed the malaise?[34]

The free donation of resources has reached a dreadful situation, where communities not only expect international NGOs to supply materials, but also to fix problems that arise out of using those resources. A pump supplied freely by an NGO would require that NGO or another to fix it, if it breaks. This is because freebies have a fundamental mental attachment to the recipient that they deserve what has been given to them or more. This is a disease. Symptoms that the disease is becoming chronic, is when people demand 'sitting allowances' in monetary forms, for attending trainings or capacity building workshops.

### d) Environment is Science, Christianity is Religion

The relationship between Christianity and science has had its own ups and downs. There are views that natural happenings in the world cannot be explained by the Bible. This is one extreme. Another extreme is to read the Bible casually and conclude that God is behind modern-day natural disasters, such as the tsunami and droughts. Some scientists despise the Bible for using a language that could be regarded as scientifically misleading. To respond to this, we need to recognize that the ancient view of the world was very different from our own and it would be anachronistic to try and read back our own scientific understanding of the working of the world and causes of natural phenomena into Biblical texts. Ecologists today realize that the world is not a static system, in which natural processes operate according to a fixed, predetermined pattern, but one that is evolving in response to a complex range of variables. The cycle of death and decay is necessary for life and the process which give rise to natural disasters are often essential to the functioning of the planet we call earth. The ancient Israelite view of how God acts within his creation is described in a very directly causal manner, in which the wind is God's messenger

---

34. Masika, *Mindset Change*, 30.

(Psalm 104:4) and the eagle soars at his command (Job 39:26). For us, reconciling contemporary scientific understanding with belief in a creator God necessitates a rethinking of emphasis and vocabulary, as suggested by Vinoth Ramachandra:

> The creator respects the integrity of his creation. The relationship between creator and creation cannot be described adequately in the language of controlling and ruling.' There is also a letting-be, a willingness to let the creation unfold in its own way and according to its intrinsic character.[35]

Max Weber's accounts on the "disenchantment of the world," reveals how Christianity played pivotal role in the construction of a modern science-based world.[36]

There is no question that science and technology have been instrumental in shaping modern society. Modern technology is at least partly to be explained as an occidental and voluntarist realizing of the Christian dogma of man's transcendence of, and rightful mastery over nature. But as we now recognize, somewhat over a century ago science and technology- hitherto quite separate activities- joined to give mankind power which, to judge by man of the ecologic effects, are out of control. If so, Christianity bears a huge burden of guilt.[37]

What is seldom said, however, is the role Christianity played shaping science and technology. It was first the Christian tradition that laid the foundations for their birth. This is viewed positively and negatively. Positively, Christianity is seen as an avenue of tremendous development that has given birth to resourceful lives that humanity is now enjoying.

---

35. Marlow, *The Earth is the Lord's*, 12.
36. Schroeder, *Max Weber and the Sociology of Culture*, 11.
37. White, Jr., "Roots of our Ecological Crisis," 1206.

### e) Do not Love the World, The Earth Could become a god!

Another erroneous world view is the eco-spirituality in which nature and humanity are seen as interconnected instead of separated, and especially that the conception that nature itself becomes to some extent sacrosanct, embodied with the divine *(Bohemen 2010)*. According to Campell:

> To accept that an indefinable absolute divine force rather than a personal, transcendent deity is the governing power in the universe is to see the whole of creation in a new light. For it is to see mankind, nature, and indeed the cosmos as a whole, as united through their shared participation in this divine force. Naturally this leads to a new view of nature and of mankind's relationship to the natural world, with the "natural" necessarily acquiring some of the attributes of the sacred.[38]

The idea that a close connection exists between nature and humans should logically provide for more concerns for the welfare of nature. Such an eco-spiritual holistic understanding is most often associated with New Age spirituality.[39]

Moreover, such a holistic worldview is seen as a decisive factor that distinguishes New Age from Christianity. Viewed from this position it would not be as self-evident to expect to find an eco-spiritual conception of nature among Christians (see however, Kearns, 1996; 1997). As such we expect that the outlined distinction between a dualistic and a holistic conception of nature will have its continuation in differences in environmental concern between Christians and New Agers. Accordingly, we expect that a form of eco-spiritual holism is much more to be found among New Agers than among Christians. This worldview is erroneous because it leads to the worship of creation rather than the creator. God's act of creation is an action of something of his very nature- it reveals his own creativity. Just as an artist or musician or poet pours something of their very selves into the work they produce,

---
38. Campbell, *The Easternization of the West*, 74.
39. Ibid.

so the creation bears something of the stamp of God. This is not to say that the creation itself is God. There is a clear distinction between regarding the natural world as divine (a characteristic of pantheism, the view that the universe or nature is divine, but not of biblical Christianity) and rediscovering the sacred nature of creation which leads us to worship the creator afresh. In relation to this, Stan Chu Ilo posits:

> Respecting the environment does not mean considering material or animal nature more important than man. Rather, it means not selfishly considering nature to be at the complete disposal of our own interests, for future generations also have the right to reap its benefits and to exhibit towards nature the same responsible freedom that we claim for ourselves.[40]

## f) This earth will be destroyed anyway

Another erroneous world view is the pessimism associated with the doctrine that the earth will be destroyed, and so we should not waste our time conserving it. The people holding this view peg their assumption on their interpretation of 2 Peter 3 to argue that this earth will be destroyed by fire. Extremists in this view, as Marlow depicts, "advocate the speeding of the return of Christ by using up the earth's resources."[41] Hillary Marlow responds to this perspective of destruction by fire in three ways. Firstly, the fact that the imagery of burning by fire does not necessarily mean destruction. The contextual meaning presented by Peter from his first epistle (1:7), and even that presented by Paul (I Corinthians 3:13), is that fire signifies purification of what was originally polluted. Secondly, the comparison of the coming fire, with the flood punishment in Genesis reveals the same purpose and result in both. In the flood story in Genesis, the earth was not totally obliterated, but the sinful humanity, and other forms of life were wiped

---

40. Ilo, *Church and Development in Africa*, 76.
41. Marlow, *The Earth is the Lord's*, 23.

out, and the earth technically recreated through water. If this is the comparison in 2 Peter 3, it follows therefore the work of the fire will be the same, to remove what is evil, and allow recreation of what is holy by God himself. Thirdly, the use of term 'new heaven and new earth,' (new= *kainos*) suggests "perfected" rather than "other." Verlyne D Verbrugge state that in classical Greek, *kainos* tends to denote what is "qualitatively new as compared with what has existed until now, what is better than the old."[42] The new earth thereby means a renewed, a better in quality than what we have, not something totally fresh, since the word *neos* would have been used instead.

Even with the impending coming of Christ, Paul addressed the retrogressive mentality of refusing to work because Christ is coming back anyway. Paul promoted the idea of positive work ethic, even saying that those who do not work should also not eat. Some international Non-Governmental Organizations have wreaked havoc in Africa, by promising utopia without making clear to the people the work ethic that utopia demands.

Another assertive argument on the fate of the material earth is provided by John O'Keefe.[43] John J. O'Keefe discusses the future reality of the material earth, and how that understanding of the eschaton informs Christian worldview and role on earth. O'keefe, realizes that many Christians have historically been nurtured to think that the earth is of no eternal value, and so, they should focus on their immaterial spiritual self, which will ultimately matter. This worldview is called the "spiritual ascent" mindset. The Christians who hold this view, for centuries, have suggested that "salvation begins in the body and ends in the spirit."[44] In their view, a clear dualism exists; eternal split, separating the material from the spiritual. The material is viewed as only a temporary hold; a preparation for what is eternal—the spiritual. Their description of the eschaton is with imagination of "white and bright. . . clouds

42. Verbrugge, *New International Dictionary of New Testament Theology*, 280.

43. O'Keefe, "Creation, Incarnation, and Resurrection," 49.

44. O'Keefe, "Creation, Incarnation, and Resurrection," 50.

and other things thin and lofty."[45] The future, according to this view, is filled with imagination of escape; from this material world, to the spiritual heaven and bliss, where they swim in the clouds dressed in white gowns, never again to touch the soil, the plants, the rocks, the water, and the animals of the earth. In O'Keefe's evaluation, this is gnostic worldview, which predates Christianity, and has its roots in Platonic thinking. To the Gnostics, there was a constant battle between matter and spirit; with the goal of salvation being "to liberate the spirit from the matter, so that it could return home."[46] Gnosticism was however heretical in most of their assumptions and was entirely rejected by the Church. The basis for rejecting Gnosticism, however, exposed the Church to positions that emphasized dualism even further. O'Keefe discusses two opposing responses of the Church Fathers, that were both against Gnosticism, but which looked at the matter, in two different lights: Irenaeus and Origen. Origen argued that matter and spirit were purposefully created by God in the beginning. God created the matter to house the spirit. When God decides to destroy matter, the spirit would just escape the matter, and go back home to God. To be in the body, for Origen, was to be 'spirits' temporarily embodied in the 'matter' waiting to be liberated for a wholly spiritual destiny. For Origen, true destiny of the human was a spiritual destiny; thus, the spirit will ascent. O'Keefe uses the analogy of Paul Santimire that this motif is like the experience of Moses in Mount Sinai, who goes to the mountain to meet God, and for a moment, is "lost in the mystery of divine power and otherness."[47] Christian who hold this worldview get immersed into the idea of the future reality of meeting God, up in the mountain, and like Moses, vanishing and escaping out of the earth; performing the spiritual ascent, to "slip the surly bonds of earth. . . and . . .touch the face of God."[48] It is understandable why people who hold this

---

45. Ibid., 50.
46. Ibid, 54.
47. Ibid, 60.
48. O'Keefe, "Creation, Incarnation, and Resurrection," 61.

view, would be difficult to influence to participate in the processes of environmental stewardship and management.

The challenge with the 'spiritual ascent' view, in O'Keefe's perspective, is that it exposes Christianity to negative critique from non-Christian environmentalist, and paints Christian faith in bad light, as being unconcerned; too heavenly minded to be of any earthly use. Furthermore, the Christian idea of evolution towards spirit in this view, "makes it possible for humans to adopt exploitative attitudes towards the natural world, because they think of themselves as, deep down really belonging to another dimension of reality and because they see this world and this life as something they need to get through."[49] O'Keefe notes that the reasoning behind 'spiritual ascent' is thus incorrect, unbiblical, and dangerous to implementation of the stewardship mandate. To show how the dualism is incorrect, he presents the theological response of Irenaeus to Gnosticism.

O'Keefe argues that the correct biblical understanding of the future of the earth, lies on the theology of Irenaeus who views material and the spirit as one, designed so from the creation. In God's master plan, Irenaeus indicates, the creation existed as physical and spiritual; and together good, until sin corrupted everything. In this plan, God executes salvation of the entire creation, by having Jesus die on the cross. In the new heaven and the new earth, which is viscerally material, humans will commune with God on the earth, and there will be plants and animals, mountains and rivers. The new heaven and the new earth will be spiritual and material. On that day, when God establishes the new heaven and a new earth, Christ's work of redeeming the creation, of setting it free from the process of decay, will be realized. This view, that God is going to renew the material earth, so that it will be good again, as it was in the beginning, is what Paul Santimire calls, the ecological motif. This is different from the spiritual ascent motif, championed by Origen and many Christians in the history of the Church. The ecological motif has imagery of the journey to the Promised Land, where the end is settlement on the fertile land, and enjoying milk

49. Ibid., 50.

and honey; a land that drinks water from heaven, and where the fruits from the trees eternally satisfy the appetites of God's people. A land where the vines produce grapes for people to make wine, and the fertile soil produce wheat for people to make bread; a land that can be touched and can be enjoyed.

O'Keefe thus concludes that the most authentic Christian teaching, the most meaningful and valid interpretation of scripture, is not 'spiritual ascent' but 'ecological motif.' Ecological motif, as O'Keefe puts it, is an expansion of liberation theology, and "orbits around a hunger and thirst for justice and the profound desire that God (should) fix what has been broken."[50] The correct view of the future is that of heavenly Jerusalem redeemed from the "wounds" it incurred as a result of the Fall, but which is teeming with life and exuberance, as it was the first day. Christians who hold this worldview, have a positive attitude about the worth of their contribution in environmental management and stewardship, because they understand that God cares about the material earth, and he will renew it, rather than destroy it.

## g) I am just one person, I cannot do much

Related to the pessimistic worldview above is another worldview that "I am just one person, I cannot do much." A person feels weak and left out alone. A story is told of a boy in the beach, trying to save lives of some sea creatures who are left in dry land by the receding tides. This missionary approaches the boy with a discouraging question: "there are millions of these creatures that will die anyway, how many can you save?" The boy is said to have responded: "I have no problem with not being able to save a million. I am only excited that I am saving some." This mind-set that "I am just one" is what Bishop Titus Masika refers to as the "grasshopper mentality."[51]

---

50. O'Keefe, "Creation, Incarnation, and Resurrection," 66.
51. Masika, *Mindset*, 86.

## Christian Worldview of Environmental Stewardship

The demand for environmental management efforts is too urgent to despise any contribution. Every personal action and contribution counts. Individual contributions may look insignificant in themselves, but when viewed collectively mean much. Furthermore, according to Ben Lowe, "the smallest of our contributions matters to God, and we should never judge its significance by how effective it appears to us in the grand scheme of things."[52] Individual contributions usually become very effective, when different individuals support each other for synergy. These individuals can then scale up their contributions by mobilizing other forces, finally forming a campaign.

---

52. Lowe, *Green Revolution*, 16.

Chapter Five

# Call for a Christian to Participate in Environmental Stewardship

> I used to think the top environmental problems were biodiversity loss, ecosystem collapse and climate change. I thought that with 30 years of good science we could address those problems. But I was wrong. The top environmental problems are selfishness, greed, and apathy... and to deal with those, we need a spiritual and cultural transformation—and we scientists don't know how to do that.
>
> —Gus Speth

## INTRODUCTION

One of the powerful motivations for any Christian to participate in an activity, is the relationship that activity has with their faith. In this sense, religion is very powerful. The conviction that one is being called by their God to act in a certain way, or to make certain sacrifice usually elicit commitment and determination that is beyond research. This explains the incomprehensible nature of

*Call for a Christian to Participate in Environmental Stewardship*

terrorism, which continues to baffle security and intelligent forces of even the developed nations.

This potential drive inherent in many religious people could be used for a good cause. Linking environmental adaptation to spiritual commitment of any Christian has the potential of causing people to act beyond the ordinary. This means that, since environmental problems can also be viewed as spiritual problems, the church which usually deals with spiritual problems should take up environment as part of its ministry. This calls for rigorous and accurate exegesis of biblical injunctions will help in formulation of good and practical activities that the church can be involved in.

## DOCTRINE OF GOD AND CREATION IN RELATION TO ENVIRONMENTAL STEWARDSHIP

Scriptures linked to God as a creator of the universe include Genesis 1–2, Job 41:11, Psalms 24, John 1:1–5, Colossians 1:15–17, among others. These passages first teach that entire creation belongs to God and worships God (Psalms 24; Job 41:11). According to Dewitt (1998), God creates everything with intentions of earning worship and praise from it. The rest on the seventh day was not an afterthought. It was the goal. It is not a theological appendix to the creation account, just a conclusion of the main events. Dewitt states that it was to "bring a closure now that the main event of creating people has been reported. It intimates the purpose of creation and the cosmos. God not only sets up the cosmos to serve as his temple...He is making a rest for himself, a rest provided for by the completed cosmos."[1]

The end of the book of Psalms proclaims, "Let everything that has breath praise the Lord!" This command to worship God is addressed not just to his human creation but to other animate life. In Psalm 148 the exhortation is widened to include all creation-sun, moon, and stars, sea creatures, mountains, trees and birds, all owe their existence to him, and so are to offer him praise. The

1. DeWitt, *Caring for Creation*, 35.

Psalmist is not concerned with how these various natural elements worship the Lord, but with the part that the whole earth plays in glorifying God.[2] The creation had original blessedness and goodness that emanated from God. If Genesis chapter 1 was a poem, then the end of every stanza was the same: 'and God saw that it was good.' The blessedness is aptly demonstrated by the diversity shown. In Genesis 1:11–12, the phrase "according to their kinds" is used three times. As shown in Genesis, diversity is a key aspect of God's blessedness. It can be thus argued that, Christians' treatment of the environment show how they value and worship the creator, God.

## Doctrine of Sin in relation to Environmental Stewardship

Sin is a major theological theme in Christian theology. It is the result of broken relationship between God and humanity. This brokenness of relationship also affects human treatment of the environment. As a result, as Gus Speth observes, humanity exhibits characteristics such as 'greed,' 'consumerism,' 'selfishness,' 'carelessness' and 'neglect' towards the environment.[3] There is an underlying spiritual dissonance in the universe that makes it difficult for humanity to live within its means and in harmony with the natural system that supports their lives. In the *Laudato Si*, Pope Francis asserts:

> This sister now cries out to us because of the harm we have inflicted on her by our irresponsible use and abuse of the goods with which God has endowed her. We have come to see ourselves as her lords and masters, entitled to plunder her at will. The violence present in our hearts, wounded by sin, is also reflected in the symptoms of sickness evident in the soil, in the water, in the air and in all forms of life. This is why the earth herself, burdened

2. Marlow, *The Earth is the Lord's*, 2008.
3. Speth, "Living on Earth," 1.

> and laid waste, is among the most abandoned and maltreated of our poor; she "groans in travail.[4]

The consequence of human action therefore, has been "the groaning of creation" (Romans 8:22). Even in the Old Testament, the prophets (Jeremiah 12:4; Hosea 4:1) described the earth as moaning.[5] According to Ben Lowe (2009), sin kills the 'shalom' that was there from the beginning. A careful reading and analysis of the Old Testament reveals that this shalom comes as a result of positive relationships between God, humanity and non-human creation. He posits:

> Shalom is the Hebrew word for peace. Meaning more than simply absence of conflict, however, it is about right relationships between God and everything else, where wholeness and flourishing occurs without opposition. Such Shalom was present in the Garden of Eden and its complete restoration is what we eagerly anticipate in the kingdom of God.[6]

Cornelius Plantinga Jr. points out that whatever opposes God's intentions and violates his shalom, is sin. The Fall of Man in Genesis resulted in death, not just of humanity but also of relationship.[7] The original shalom was positive relationship between God, humanity and non-human creation. Hillary Marlow graphically represents this in triangular version where God, humans, and non-human creation relate very well in a give and take scenario.[8] God satisfy humans, and humans serve God. God sustains non-human creation, and in return he receives glory and worship. Human relationship to non-human creation is described in terms of stewardship and in return humans receive satisfaction. Lowe observes that "all three levels of human relationships-with God, with

---

4. Pope Francis, *Laudato Si'*, 2.
5. Marlow, *The Earth is the Lord's*, 10.
6. Ibid, 27.
7. Plantinga Jr., *Not the Way it is Supposed to Be*, 1.
8. Marlow, *The Earth is the Lord's*, 9.

one another, and creation, are being violated."[9] Prophets such as Micah, Amos, and Isaiah advocated for justice and righteousness and for the restoration of God's purpose for human relationships, his shalom in the world. What is not so often noted is that the absence of these core values in society results in disruption to the land, including drought and failed harvests (Micah 6:15; Amos 5:11) and more widespread devastation of the physical landscape (Amos 8:7–8; Isaiah 1:7–8). If the humans would sin by neglecting God's fundamental principles of justice and righteousness, there are consequences in the wider environment.

This being the case, the most careful science and the best economic theories and the most profound governmental policies, while necessary, will never be enough. Spiritual problem demands a spiritual solution.[10] The Church's mission therefore of fighting sin, means that when God forgives human sin and blesses the earth, environmental health is also realized. Ecclesial participation in this aspect is related to the ministry of preaching for holy living and creating awareness that God's promise of blessing the earth, is a gift that accompanies forgiveness to repentant sinners.

## Doctrine of Humanity and Environmental Stewardship

The third doctrine that has been given prominence in theology is what is commonly known as "the doctrine of Man." It has been widely accepted that humanity is central to the entire creation.

## Doctrine of Humanity verses Dominion and Anthropocentricism

The whole creation is recorded to have looked "very good" to God only after Adam and Eve had entered the scene. Some commentators have argued that this statement suggests that there is something that only humanity could add to make the entire creation

9. Lowe, *Green Revolution*, 9.
10. Brown, *Our Father's World*, 26.

'very good.' This therefore means that humanity means a lot even to God. Ironically, scathing attack levelled against Christianity by Lynn White in 1967 is related to the doctrine of humanity. White Jr., using passages related to commissioning of Adam in Genesis 1–2, accused Christian teaching of anthropocentricism and dominion as being the cause of environmental degradation. Does the doctrine of humanity really advocate for anthropocentrism and destructive dominion? The following section examines the interpretation of the passages used as reference for these positions.

## Dominion

God declares in Genesis 1 to Adam and Eve,

> "Be fruitful and increase in number; fill the earth and subdue it. Rule over the fish of the sea and the birds of the air and over every living creature that moves on the ground" (Genesis 1:28).

This has been interpreted by others to mean that humanity was given uncensored freedom to exploit the environment. One such conclusion was made by Lynn White Jr. in 1967. Such conclusions mean that Christians destroy the environment lawfully, based on an alleged biblical permission. A careful study of the contextual meaning of the word dominion, used, reveal otherwise. It reveals that, as Robert Manahan observes, human beings are to rule over the earth and nature, but he is to be a biblical ruler who is modelled after Jesus Christ, a servant king (Mark 10:45), who keeps and protects the environment.[11] The idea was for human beings to obey God even in their actions on nature. Nature was to obey humanity as humanity obeys God. God was to be beneficent to humanity as humanity becomes beneficent to nature. In Genesis 2:15 Adam was to work and care for the land, as an elaboration of an instruction he was given to have dominion. Adam was created in the image of God, and so expected to use what God had provided, to bring forth beauty and accomplishment to the creation

11. Manahan, "Christ as the Second Adam, 12.

of God. Other scriptures pointing out to stringent expectation of a human being include the book of Deuteronomy 23:13 where there is guidance provided for the disposal of human waste, and in Exodus, guidance is given on the rest that the land should get. In Deuteronomy, guidance is given in the use of land, and trees (Deuteronomy 20:19–20).

A human being was therefore not just the last created being, but a co-creator with God, with assigned responsibility to care and maintain the created blessedness. This theme of human responsibility to care for the environment is maintained throughout the Bible. The doctrine of man advocates for stewardship mindset. Human beings are to care for what belongs to God.

## *Anthropocentricism*

According to John Calvin, "the end for which all things were created was that none of the convenience and necessities of life might be wanting to men."[12] In this view, humanity is portrayed as being the center of creation. In this book, this view is understood as anthropocentricism. Anthropocentricism is a human centered perspective of the entire creation, positioning a human being as being the very reason creation exists. A careful study of the Genesis 1 however reveals that man is positioned as a steward, rather than a 'god' to be revered by the creation. Arguing against anthropocentricism, Hillary Marlow asserts:

> Such a human-centred perspective on God's world seems to take little account of the diversity, complexity and, to our minds, strangeness of much of the natural world, which is now accessible to us through a wealth of nature films and documentaries. But it also carries a more profound theological weakness affecting our view of God as well as of the world and can lead us to a self-centred and childish understanding of God as the one who always gives us whatever we want. If we see the rest of the world- the 'non-human creation'- as existing purely for human

12. Calvin, *Institutes*, 22.

## Call for a Christian to Participate in Environmental Stewardship

benefit, we fail to take seriously either the creation or its creator. Such attitudes have contributed to exploitative and damaging practice in many parts of the world, as human beings have tried to take what they regarded as their right, without regard for the consequences.[13]

Anthropocentricism is therefore a view that is totally against the Biblical teaching. Today our planet faces an environmental crisis wrought by the ever-increasing demands and changes of its human population. Ironically it is this same humanity which God designated to care for the earth, not to destroy it.

## The Place of a Human Being in Environmental Stewardship

Humankind, both male and female are created in the 'image of God.' In addition, they are given special instructions to subdue and have dominion over the animals Genesis 1:27–28). Other scripture clearly show that he is made "a little lower than angels and crowned with glory and honour" (Psalms 8:5). For many Christians this suggests that human beings are regarded as separate from creation, and totally distinct from other created beings. An examination of all factors however reveals otherwise. For example, the fact that Adam is created, in the same day as other animals, and using *adamah*, the dust of the earth, shows that he was part of the creation. Dyke adds that God created the universe in such a way that humans are inseparably linked to it, physically as well as spiritually.[14] Out of the common stuff of earth God formed a man: "The Lord God formed the man from the dust of the ground, and breathed into his nostrils the breath of life and the man became a living being" (Genesis 2:7).

The implication of this is that Adam is presented as being part of the creation. For some scholars, the implication of 'dust' is that he is made from nothing. For other scholars, he is made from

---

13. Ibid, 5.
14. Dyke, Mahan, Sheldon, & Brand, *Redeeming Creation*, 14.

soil, that is, what had already been made, to show he is physically connected to the ground. Hillary Marlow points out:

> In Genesis 2, the focus narrows to the formation of a single human being (*ha-adam*, "the human') and his purpose in the wider creation. The earth is depicted as ground (*adamah*) without water and without vegetation (v 5–6), but once rain has fallen, the Lord God moulds the human from the dust of the ground and places him in a garden, the Garden of Eden. This humble origin, graphically conveyed by the shared Hebrew root of the word '*adam*' from the *adamah*, to mean human from the humus, is one that the human being shares with the vegetation (v 9) as well as with other animals (v 19). In today's scientific terms, it is a reminder that we are just one of the carbon-based life forms which colonize this planet.[15]

Therefore, human beings should understand their position, not as superior, but as responsible. Adam was given the responsibility to rule over what God had made. He is to rule from among, not above. This position makes a human being both advantaged and accountable. Advantaged in terms of the opportunity to provide for his pleasure from what God has created. Accountable in terms of the expectations to make decisions, and be ready to answer questions concerning those decisions, when the owner comes to ask. The expectations therefore is that Adam was to rule like how Christ rules the Church, not to get pleasure, but to develop and give meaning. Humanity is called apart, to image God in caring for the earth and its creatures. They are to "subdue and rule over" but also to "work and take care of" (Genesis 2.15). This perspective should suffice to deal effectively with two dangerous worldviews: anthropocentrism and dominion.

---

15. Marlow, *The Earth is the Lord's*, 18.

*Call for a Christian to Participate in Environmental Stewardship*

## God's intention of Adam in Environmental Stewardship

Millard Erickson asserts that proper definition of the term "*adam*" (which was also given as a name for the first male human being), reveals that God had the entire humanity in mind, when he provided natural resources for his consumption and enjoyment. Erickson observes that Adam was a definite historical individual, but nevertheless, he and his wife Eve were the entire human race at that point. Adam contained within him, germinally or seminally, all humans who ever will be within the span of history. God did not promise and provide to Adam alone the rest of creation for consumption. God did not intend for Adam alone to enjoy its benefits. God intended for all the benefits to accrue to all members of the human race, at all times.[16] This thus requires a stewardship mentality.

According to Marlow, it can be argued that, whatever God intended for Adam and Eve in creation, whatever view he had on them, whatever plans he had in mind, these would be for all humanity as well. What did God intend for Adam? First, as Marlow observes, Adam was created to be a steward. He was to care for the created system, so that everything would benefit. The various parts of the creation are interconnected and thus have interdependency with and upon one another. The fortunes of one part of the universe are tied up with those of other parts. The humans depend directly and indirectly on the other creatures and should not in any way tamper with the system.[17]

The ideal stewardship role of humanity, as John Calvin asserts, is closely related to the attitude of contentment. He posits:

> The custody of the garden was given to Adam, to show that we possess the things which God has committed to our hands, on the condition, that being content with the frugal and moderate use of them, we should take care of what shall remain. Let him who possesses a field, so partake of its yearly fruits, that he may not suffer the ground

16. Erickson in Land & Moore, *The Earth Is the Lord's*, 2.
17. Marlow, *The Earth is the Lord's*, 9.

> to be injured by negligence; but let him endeavour to hand it down to posterity as he received it, or even better cultivated. Let him so feed on its fruits, that he neither dissipates it by luxury, nor permits it to be marred or ruined by neglect... Let everyone regard himself as the steward of God in all things which he possesses.[18]

The word 'stewardship' as used in the Old Testament means being in-charge of a house (Genesis 43:19; 44:4; Isaiah 22:15). In the New Testament a steward, *epitropos* (Matthew 20:8; Galatians 4:2) is the one who has been put on trust or honour to care or guard something. Stewardship *oikonomos* (Luke 16:2–3; 1 Corinthians 4:1–2; Titus 1:7; 1 Peter 4:10), refers to the act of honouring the owner of the house, by having the right relationships within the home, in relationship to an owner, for who stewardship is performed.[19] Stewardship therefore is acting in God's love to do activities that enhance God's creation in a way that brings honour to Him. This is done first in recognition that harmony, unity, purity and integrity in creation is important to elicit a respect for creation. Secondly, these activities are done to show love to an ailing environment for its own good. As Francis Schaeffer states, it is the biblical view of nature that gives nature a value in itself. It involves responsible behaviour and lifestyle against greed and consumerism behaviour.[20]

The participants of stewardship are Christians who are in the covenant relationship with God. It does not mean that the people should be rich or get sponsored by big organizations. Christians need to use whatever is available, learning from the staff of Moses, and the widow's oil in II Kings 4:1–7. Edward Brown asserts that Christians need to care for the environment more than anyone else, because they have relationships with the creator.[21] The proper approach to creation care should be theologically sound, scientifically informed and implemented by a community of redeemed

18. Calvin in Sorley, *Christ and Creation*, 63.
19. DeWitt, *Caring for Creation*, 44.
20. Schaeffer & Middleman, *Pollution and the Death of Man*, 43.
21. Brown, *Our Father's World*, 79.

people acting out of love for God and for each other. The bar of performance for the Church of course, is higher than is expected of others. The First epistle of John 3:5 state that anyone who claims to know Jesus Christ should also walk in his light. As discussed earlier, Jesus is creator, integrator, and reconciler. Ironically, many who call on his name abuse, neglect, and do not give care about creation. Yet many Christians have not even come to a level where they consider these things carefully, to wonder how they honor God the creator verbally, yet fail to do God's work practically; how they praise God from whom all blessings flow, yet diminish and destroy God's creatures on earth; how they learn at the Church that God created all things in a good condition, yet participate in destructive behavior. Calvin DeWitt summarizes this contradiction precisely: The pieces of this puzzle do not fit! One piece says, "We honor the Great Master!" The other piece says, "We despise his great master pieces!"[22] Ecclesial participation in environmental stewardship come because of proper theological understanding of the doctrine of Man, that he is created, not to be 'god' or have destructive dominion, over the creation, but to care for the earth, so that everything teems with blessedness and goodness.

The article by Dermot A. Lane (2017) provides a discussion on anthropological and teleological reflections on *Laudato Si*.[23] In his argument, Lane notes that modernity seen humans declaring their independence from reality, and have behaved with absolute dominion; domination marked by an excessive human centeredness, anthropocentrism which compromises the intrinsic dignity of the natural world. In order to be useful in solving the ecological crisis, Lane interprets *Laudato Si*, as having guidance on how humans need to be decentered in order to be reconnected with a larger scheme of things. Humans need to receive a new understanding of interconnectedness, where everything created by God depends and supports each other. "To exist," Lane avers, "is always

---

22. DeWitt, *Caring for Creation*, 16.

23. Lane, "Anthropological and Theological Reflections on Laudato Si," 45.

to coexist, and to be is to be in relation, to being is always being towards" (39).

Lane observes that at some instance, some human worldview has emerged, positioning humans as being 'other' than creation of God, but as being the object of God's creation; that everything was created for them, and humans are at the centre. This mindset, according to Lane's interpretation of *Laudato Si'*, is to blame in the current environmental crisis. A better view, proposed by Pope Francis, is for humans to understand that they are part of nature, included in it and thus in constant interaction with it. It is this view that is to blame when humans developed an exaggerated sense of importance assuming a license to exploit the earth's resources.

Lane also discusses the role of the Holy Spirit in the creation. In addition to what many people understand the Holy Spirit to do in relation to spiritual gifts seen in the New Testament, Lane avers that the Holy Spirit should also be understood as having been present and active from creation. Lane avers:

> There are a number of points worth noting about these opening verses of the Bible. First of all, the breath of God, the spirit of God, is involved at the very beginning, at the dawn of time. Secondly, we are told that the sport of God 'swept over the face of the earth.' A netter translation would be that the Spirit of God was brooding over the earth, or hatching over the earth, or warming the earth like the mother hen in a nest.[24]

In this argument, Lane shows that there is an intimate link then, between God (Holy Spirit) and the creation, in respect to the Spirit of God, hatching over everything, as the hen does so to the chicks. The earth is 'hatched' by the Spirit of God, just as humans are also hatched. To show how humans are also intimately linked to the creation, Lane uses the second creation story in Genesis 2.

In the second creation story in Genesis 2, Lane describes the position of a human being, Adam, that was created from the earth, *adamah*. Overall, Lane show the link that is there between Holy

24. Lane, "Anthropological and Theological Reflections on Laudato Si," 45.

Spirit, nature and human beings. Humans and the entire creation are 'En-Spirited.' Lane interestingly links Christ also into the web. He states:

> The Word of God, enfleshed in Jesus is therefore, linked to the whole of humanity and the wider community of life on earth that has its origins in the evolution of the cosmos. If we can appreciate the human as cosmic dust in a state of consciousness and, therefore, every human being as a child of the cosmos, including Jesus, then we should be able to appreciate the Word (Logos) wedded to the human, to the flesh of the earth and the dust of cosmos. The incarnation reaches into the core of humanity and the heart of the creation.[25]

In this quote, Lane thus finds and shows how linkages between human, creation, Holy Spirit, and Christ helps to establish a good understanding of relationships, and to affirm that humans, and indeed the entire creation were creation for relationships. This view of human if understood, will have the potential to prevent unbridled exploitation of the earth's resources, by people, especially Christians.

## The Doctrine of 'Covenant' in relation to Environmental Stewardship

One biblical injunction that clearly demonstrate environmental problem requiring spiritual solution is II Chronicles 7:14 which state: If my people, who are called by my name, will humble themselves and pray and seek my face and turn from their wicked ways, then will I hear from heaven and will forgive their sin and will heal their land. How does God bring this healing? It is evident from scripture, that God brings healing as a gift that accompanies his covenantal promise to repentant hearts. God has a covenant with his people, where he is the suzerain king, while humanity is

---

25. Ibid.

# Christian Faith and Environmental Stewardship

the vassal. To understand the suzerain-vassal relationship in a covenant, an examination of Hebrew covenants will help.

The Bible has several covenants made between God and specific characters or people groups, for example Noahic, Abrahamic and Davidic covenants (Genesis 6:18; 9:12; 17:7; 2 Samuel 7). A covenant is a contract, usually between two parties. According to Sonja Page, biblical covenants are modelled on practices of the societies of the first and second millennium B. C. in the Ancient Near East.[26] In the Old Testament times, common covenants were between suzerain and vassal kings. The suzerain king initiated the covenant, and came up with stipulations, sanctions, promises, and for obeying the covenant, and even punishment that would follow in case of disobedience. The Hebrew word for covenant, *berith* has a connotation of agreement between two parties, where both commit to honour their contracts. Like other Ancient Near Eastern treaties, God followed the same pattern when making his covenants with his chosen leaders and Israel. The terms of covenants included the suzerain king providing the stipulations for the covenant. The initiative for making the covenant came from the suzerain king, and so were the other parts of the covenant: stipulations, promises of blessing or curses. In the Biblical covenants, God provided instructions to be followed by his people, with blessings for either obeying and curses for disobeying the instructions. The promises of blessings to certain individuals or people groups, demonstrates God's witness to his faithfulness and nature.

In the covenant that God made with the Israelites, the judgement for either blessings or curses depended directly on the quality of their response to God's covenant. The sanction was so clear and the promise of blessing so attractive, that the Israelites did not need a reminder of the consequence that would befall them if they disobeyed. Even in the case of Abraham, obedience to God's instruction gave him blessings. When Israelites became disobedient, their promise of blessing was lifted, and replaced with curses, where their land 'vomited them' out into exile. The land motif runs all through the Old Testament, with clear communication of the possibility of

26. Page, Biblical Land Covenants, 1.

*Call for a Christian to Participate in Environmental Stewardship*

loss in case of disobedience. It is possible that the Israelites did not believe that such a loss of land could ever happen. The last deportation of Israelites to exile, in fact included the King of Judah (II Kings 25). After seventy years of exile, some leaders decided to repent, and to lead others in the same. God remembered his promise, and so Israelites could return to Judah. Ezra reminded the Israelites returning from exile about God's covenant, showing clearly God's stipulations, promises of either blessings or curses, depending on their response. Ezra reports that his audience were 'appalled' and stood from sunrise to midday, listening to God's law, and wondering how they became blatantly disobedient. To them it was clear that God was just in whatever had befallen them.

God's stipulations stressed clearly that continuing possession of the Promised Land dependent entirely upon their faithfulness to God (Deuteronomy 11:8–12). Some Israelites wavered in their trust and obedience along the way towards the Promised Land. The punishment for them was that they would not inherit the land. According to Presbyterian Eco-Justice Task Force, (1989) Israel's greatest sin was breaking of the covenant they had entered with God in two major ways: idolatry and injustice. Israel was expected to worship God alone, but this was not kept. They were expected to treat their neighbours and the earth with justice but this they also failed. Amos addresses those "who trample upon the needy and bring the poor of the land to an end" (Amos 8:4).

The curses that befell Israel for disobedience were devastating to individuals and their nation in similar proportions. Sadly, the punishment and curses also affected the land, resulting in environmental degradation. Presbyterian Eco-Justice Task Force observes that "a degraded environment is regarded as punishment for a basic stance of disobedience –unfaithfulness to the covenant."[27]

Ken Gnanakan observes that the connection between land and God-Israel relation clearly communicated to Israel that God was the owner of the land.[28] In fact, God says 'the land is mine and

27. Presbyterian Eco-Justice Task Force, *Keeping and Healing the Creation*, 48.

28. Gnanakan, *Responsible Stewardship of God's Creation*, 60.

you are but aliens and my tenants' (Leviticus 25:23); and He refers to it clearly as 'my land' (Jeremiah 2:7; 16:18). The Hebrew word *nahalah* is used in 2 Samuel 20:19, and 21:3 means that land was loaned to Israel but was still owned by God (Deuteronomy 25:23). The lending of the land is a covenant God made, with obligations and expectations. Right from the beginning, God communicated clearly that the land was a gift (Genesis 12:1, 17:4–8). In Deuteronomy 9:6, God clearly states: "Know, then, that the Lord your God is not giving you this good land to occupy because of your righteousness; for you are a stubborn people." This thus means was given as a gift of grace, not deserved by the Israelites (Leviticus 25).

Gnanakan therefore observes that no one was free to do as he liked with the land.[29] Israel received clear communication on how they were to handle the gift of God, and the repercussion for treating it as the owner wanted. Their ongoing occupancy depended on their "moral behaviour" and their "observance of the law."[30] Moses made it clear in the book of Deuteronomy 11 that Israel needed to pay attention to the Commandments of God to enjoy his blessings of inheriting the land. In addition, their obedience would guarantee them long life in the land. The long life is because God was going to give them lives in abundance. The symbolism used was that the land would be flowing with milk and honey, a powerful way of illustrating abundant living that God was promising. God would crown his blessings by sending them rain to water their crops. God makes it clear that his blessings of rain would by far be better than foot pump irrigation that they were used to doing in Egypt. God would just bring rain in the right time. The Israelites would not worry again about security, because God was going to watch over the land from the beginning of the year to its end. God would not be like the Egyptians gods who were consulted only during planting season and harvest. God promised to watch over the land every day of the year. The implication was that if Israelites were obedient to God, they would be assured of blessings and happiness in the land that God was giving them as a gift.

29. Ibid., 62.
30. Ibid.

The land they were to inherit was a land of freedom, abundance, and fulfilment, flowing with milk and honey. Furthermore, to show clearly that God was present in this land, Israelites were given directions on how to inhabit the land well. They were to give their newly acquired land a sabbatical rest, on the seventh year, where the land was to lie fallow for a whole year. Their people were also supposed to be concerned about the poor and the afflicted. (Ibid) They posit:

> God's redemption is twofold: to free the weak and oped from unjust conditions, and to free all sinners (including us) from violating others and for our own authentic humanity. God thus restores human creatures to health and wholeness, and at the heart of the matter is the forgiveness of sin. . . The forgiving redeemer frees us, not for withdrawal from this world and contemplation of another, and not for community with our own kind only, but for right relationships with all of God's creation.[31]

## The Doctrine of Christ in relation to Environmental Stewardship

One of the passages used to argue for divinity of Jesus is Colossians 1:15–18, where Christ is clearly shown as the creator, 'sustainer,' and redeemer of the earth. The understanding of the role of Christ in creation and sustenance is assumed in this chapter to be clear. However, the role of Christ in redemption is perceived to be least understood and is therefore given more attention. Matthew 19:28 and Romans 8:21–22 show that Christ will redeem the earth from the current form of decay and will liberate it from the bondage it now suffers. How will this liberation happen? Revelation 21:1 states: "then I saw a new heaven and a new earth, for the first heaven and the first earth had passed away, and there was no longer any sea." Does the new heaven and the new earth mean that the current earth will be wiped away? To understand this, we need to

---

31. Gnanakan, *Responsible Stewardship of God's Creation*, 50.

look at another passage: Isaiah 65. In this passage, Isaiah presents a picture of the millennium, where human beings, non-human creation, and God will be living together on the earth harmoniously, and even the serpent will 'lie with a baby" peacefully. Christ thus shall restore relationships in the new earth. The word used for this restoration, *apekatestathee*, is also used in Luke 6:10 in the healing of a hand. Jesus did not procure another hand but restored the 'corrupted' hand to a condition considered 'good.' This means that, rather than procuring a new earth, the ministry of Jesus will be to correct the corruption of the current earth and restore relationships. If Christ shall restore the earth, into an original good situation, does not this action bring to question the morality of those who corrupted the earth in the first place? Should it also not excite people to begin to care for the environment now, since they are participating in the process of healing? John receives a revelation where God was seen fellowshipping with humanity in a similar situation as was in Eden: 'in the coolness of the evening.' This idea is useful in moving people to participate in the work of restoration now.

## ECCLESIAL PARTICIPATION

The forgoing discussions have demonstrated that scriptural passages used as reference for key doctrines in Christianity, also provide guidance for environmental stewardship. Christian theology therefore, can be used to influence ecclesial participation in environmental actions. The causal mechanism can be graphically represented as below:

| Positive Theological understanding | → | Ecclesial Participation |

| Doctrine of God: God created the earth so that the creation would worship him | Christian treatment of the earth's resources should be done in such a way that the creation remains blessed and in good condition to continue worshipping God. |
| Doctrine of Sin: Sin has broken the relationship between God, Humanity and non-human creation | The church should lead repentant behaviour, and preach for repentance and holiness to attract God's blessing of the land |
| Doctrine of Humanity: Humanity has a divine responsibility to be stewards of the environment | The Church should demonstrate stewardship behaviour in their activities, rather than exercise destructive dominion, or portray anthropocentrism |
| Doctrine of Covenant: God has a covenant with humanity, if kept, the earth will be blessed. | Christians should treat the land as a gift, in a way that honours the giver—God. The church should create awareness that holy living attracts God's blessing on the earth, and that corruption and injustice will bring curses, such as drought. |
| Doctrine of Christ: Christ is the creator, sustainer, and redeemer of creation | If Christ shall restore the earth, into an original good situation, Christians should not corrupt it, and should seek to participate in restorative activities as a way of honouring Christ |

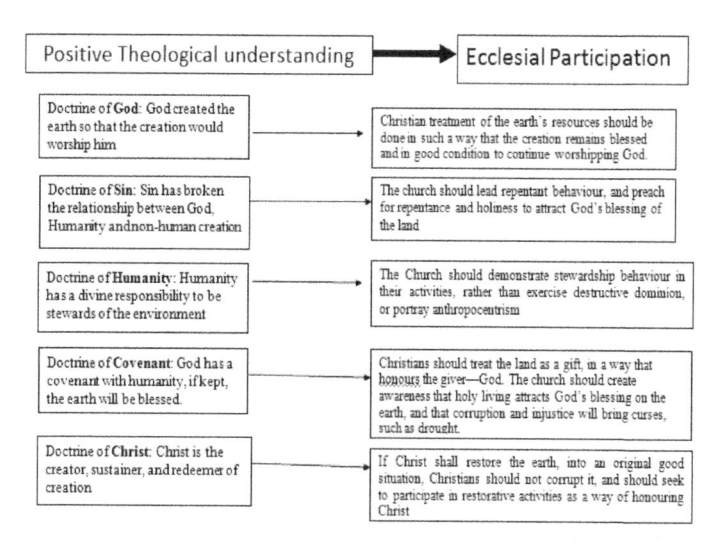

**Figure 6: Ecclesial Participation Causal Mechanism**

The diagram above shows that if the Church has the right theological understanding, and properly formed Christian worldview, it would participate in environmental stewardship. Kenya with a population of 45 million, and where majority are Christians, would have majority of its citizens participating in actions. George Kinoti points out specific areas of Christian involvement:

> [w]e must work to rescue all creatures in danger of extinction—whether the danger comes from pollution, habitat change, overfishing, poaching or any other cause. Christians should be encouraged to take proper care of their own fields or gardens and to participate in community protection of common water and grazing resources. Christians should also support national and international policies and laws to govern the care of the environment and the use of natural resources. We should be working alongside people like Wangari Maathai, the Kenyan woman who was awarded the Nobel Peace Prize because of her work to conserve Africa's environment.[32]

---

32. Kinoti

In other words, Christians all over the country should, as a form of worshipping God, practice water and soil conservation, planting and caring for the trees, do waste management and even preach and teach about environmental stewardship in the churches and Christian meetings. They should also develop a conservation mindset and stewardship perspectives that will impel them to reduce the resources they consume and reuse or recycle what they have not used.

## CONCLUSION

This chapter has discussed how various scriptural references to key Christian doctrines also provide guidance to environmental stewardship. The doctrine of 'Creation' shows that everything that was created belongs to God and was first blessed by God. Therefore, human beings should treat it with the same respect they have for God and should ensure that in their treatment of the environment, the blessedness is not compromised. The doctrine of 'Sin' also shows that, irresponsible human actions towards the environment is a demonstration of corruption inherited from the Fall of Man, a temptation that any redeemed Christian should seek to overcome. God's covenant with humanity requires obedience to God, and the reward is that the land will be blessed. The chapter has also shown that the mission of Christ to save and redeem mankind is tied with his mission to redeem the environment at the end (eschatology). The ministry of Jesus at the end, which includes healing of the earth, should excite people now to participate in the process.

In this chapter, it has been argued that Christian faith can influence environmental stewardship in so many ways. The world is struggling with various environmental concerns such as deforestation, pollution and scarcity of water for domestic use, global warming, droughts, degradation of agricultural lands, and species extinction. It has also argued that human actions, mostly due to poverty, corruption, or ignorance are to blame for most of these degradations. Climate change also plays a big role in exasperating the conditions in different countries. There is a direct relationship between the culture, economy, and geographical conditions of different countries, with poor corrupt countries suffering the worst environmental degradation. Erosion was also found to be exacerbated by overgrazing, especially in the case of limited land; a factor which compromised the potential of the soil to support agriculture.

Furthermore, the existing theological theses relating to environment have made several arguments. Notable ideas include the view that Christians should participate environmental adaptation practices, because environmental matters are spiritual matters also, and environmental problems are spiritual problems, with roots in human sinful nature, evident in how humans exhibit gluttony in consumption, selfishness in hoarding, and blindness in sustainability of the nature's benefits. In some instances, humans do not care about sustainability. Secondly, the church should practice environmental adaptation because in so doing, they ex respect for God the owner, just as anyone would treat materials belonging to a person they respect. Thirdly, the church should practice environmental adaptation because in so doing, they ex respect for God the owner, just as anyone would treat materials belonging to a person they respect. Again, the church should practice environmental adaptation because in so doing, they ex respect for God the owner, just as anyone would treat materials belonging to a person they respect.

Fifthly, the church should practice environmental adaptation because in so doing, they ex respect for God the owner, just as anyone would treat materials belonging to a person they respect. Sixthly Christians should practice environmental adaptation to restore the earth towards its original goodness, where its capacity to praise God was still at its quintessence. If the purpose of creating a 'good' creation was for God to enjoy the glory of good creation, shouldn't any attempt to restore such goodness be perceived as sacred? Seventhly, Christians should practice environmental adaptation to restore the earth towards its original goodness, where its capacity to praise God was still at its quintessence. If the purpose of creating a 'good' creation was for God to enjoy the glory of good creation, shouldn't any attempt to restore such goodness be perceived as sacred? Christians should also understand that humans were created, out of the dust (*adamah*), and this means essentially is that they are united to the earth. Humans, however, were given the responsibility to be stewards of God's earth. This included caring and making intelligent decisions to enhance the creation in a way that brings honor to God.

The ninth finding I found in relation to this is that God's relationship with Israel is set as an example of the ideal relationship of God with humanity. Land is loaned to humans as a gift for obedience to God. Israel was given instruction on how to treat this 'gift' so that its benefits would continue being available. The way human beings treat the land show how respectful they are to God and to other humans. Again, Christians should participate in environmental adaptation practices because Creation has value now, and in the future, and that it will not be reduced to nothingness in the future apocalyptic era but will continue being relevant. Finally, Environmental actions should be geared towards establishment of *Shalom*. God satisfy humans and humans serve God. God sustains non-human creation, and in return He receives glory and worship. Human relationship to non-human creation is described about stewardship and in return humans receive satisfaction.

CHAPTER SIX

# The Conserving Church in Kenya

When atrocities happen, it's like when the rain falls; no one shouts, 'stop it!' anymore.

—BERTOLT BRECHT

## INTRODUCTION

IN THIS CHAPTER, I discuss the Church community I envision. I present my personal reflections of what I think a modern Church in Kenya should be doing, the activities that deserve our efforts, in case we need to remain good stewards in God's sight. I seek to show that, a conserving Church, a community that deliberately and communally take up environmental stewardship with serious spiritual priority, is the champion of God's kingdom envisioned by Christ in his sermon on being the light of the world. I intend to show in this chapter that being the light of the world involves shining the love of God, so bright that the world, will see, and know the right way to go. In my view, a passive church, the church that sits in silence hoping that an angel of some kind would wake up and show people the best way to act in the society, is not helpful in Kenya, and will be regarded like the lazy servant, who did not trade with the talent, and who did not enjoy the joy of the Master's return. Professor Calvin DeWitt notes that the Church in America once lobbied for a legislation: "The Endangered Species Act." The Church campaigned for this act, terming it as "Our Noah's Ark" and ensuring that it was accorded enough media coverage, with news conference where the evangelicals testified that the issue of endangered species and species extinction was a religious one. This once in a lifetime activity by the Church in America is worth copying all over the world.[1] Since the Church has been energetic in seeking to respond to many needs that we see in the world, such as feeding the hungry, healing the sick, disaster management, et cetera, caring for the creation should not be seen as being impossible.[2] This chapter argues that in order for the Church of Christ to shine the light of God effectively, it ought to cultivate a sense of wonder at God's creation, appreciation and worship; nurture a culture of responsibility and accountability in relation to environment, develop a passion among its adherents to love knowledge, and encourage social transformation in respect to wealth and possession.

## SENSE OF WONDER AND GOD'S CREATION

Buildings, vehicles, and machines that have been made magnificently usually elicit a sense of awe and wonder and amazement, after they are completed. Sometimes, this sense of wonder is in the heart and mind of the designer; to produce an art that will make people to stop for a moment and admire their work. Conservation activities cannot be done with any honesty, until a Christian begins to see the splendor, grandeur and beauty of what is called nature, but is God's own act of creation. This will lead to a heart of gratitude and contentment when enjoying the benefits of creation,

1. DeWitt, *Caring for Creation: Responsible Stewardship of God's Handiwork*, 22.
2. Brown, *Our Father's World*, 5.

rather than gluttony corruption and incessant materialism that has characterized many people, especially in Kenya.

People who appreciate the role of God in nature, and who respond by giving offerings of thanksgiving after the harvest, are easily drawn towards environmental management. A certain community in Kenya that live in Machakos County have a ceremony they do every harvest, which is partly a celebration of harvest, and partly a giving-of-offering service. When I attended this ceremony in 2016, farmers were bringing their harvests of maize, mangoes, onions, beans, sweet potatoes, beans, honey, avocadoes, and other similar harvest. The celebration began in a farm, and gradually moved into a church that was there, partly because of need for shelter. The ceremony involved prayers of thanksgiving, testimonies of hard work, and plans for the following season. Non-Christians were invited to participate. The more people talked about what God had done for them in their farms, the more it became real for the non-Christians how God worked through people to restore both the hearts of people and their farms.

The understanding that what is commonly referred to as 'nature' is a creation of God, helps dissipate a recent and growing mentality of compartmentalizing what is spiritual and what is material. Compartmentalization puts some things such as faith in God, in one category, while material tangible objects are put in another category, and studied in science. Compartmentalization says that environmental matters, which are scientific in nature, cannot become subjects of investigation or participation in the realm of faith. Compartmentalization further says, "I am a Christian, I should stay away from matters of environment, for these earthly things will soil my relationship with God."

## CULTURE OF RESPONSIBILITY AND ACCOUNTABILITY

Successful communities in Africa are those communities that have invested in responsible behavior and accountability. Responsibility is the understanding that something needs to be done by you.

Accountability is the understanding that you will be required to explain what and why you acted in a certain way. Ordinarily, communities in Africa had unwritten rules on what to do, and what not to do in different circumstance. In case someone acted in a way that contravened the set-up rules, this person would be required to explain why.

The success of behavior change in many communities lies on how those communities establish their accountability system. In many African communities, community accountability, which is a process where individual people, families, groups, or tribes, would work together guided by certain unwritten laws to achieve a certain goal. Those who do not act in such was as expected, would always be expected to explain to the community why they were not able to do so. To be accepted and accorded respect, each member of these communities would strive to excel according to the standards already set and passed on from one generation to another. Catherine Jendia asserts that African society attaches great importance and value to accountability.[3] She defines accountability, as understood in Africa as being:

> Accountability and integrity are human social values used to distinguish what is right from what is wrong with specific reference to social behavior—that is, a person's position in society in relations to others. Accountability is allowing others to build trust in your person, your company, your executives, your actions and your vision through trust, transparency and the creation of mutual respect. Accountability is expected of both leaders and the lead in public as well as private sectors.[4]

This means that for successful leadership in Africa, establishment of accountability system will become paramount. Jendia further asserts that accountability helps people in the community to act responsibly.[5] The church, having a wide knowledge and experience dealing with various cultures, should find a way where com-

3. Jendia, Leadership, Accountability, and Integrity, 164.
4. Ibid.
5. Ibid, 167.

munities can implement accountability processes. For example, a church can teach its adherents on the importance of planting indigenous trees in Kenya and establish an accountability system where members report on what they have for a certain reward system in kind. Christian Impact Mission in Yatta Kenya have an accountability system where members of their church must dig a water pan, which holds water during rainy season, and which can be used for irrigation and domestic purposes. The accountability system is that if members do not fulfil this community condition, the church cannot allow them to participate in certain church rituals. The members of this denomination have accepted this system joyfully.

Communities valued responsible behavior, and rewarded individuals who acted responsibly. Among the Keiyo community for example, there are well-established ethos and taboos that were intended to nurture people to proper living. In this community, taboos were referred to as "*kireiywek*" and would be passed on from one generation to another. Mostly, they were things that 'one would not do, and should not ask why.' For example, it was wrong to urinate on water, and it was wrong to cut certain trees. Unfortunately, in Kenya, due to the influence of Westernization and capitalism, individuals are gradually becoming selfish, and do not think the society demands accountability from them. These taboos are now lost, disregarded, or un-respected. As a result, trees that had been left growing for centuries have been cut and sold by the young generation. It is my contention that a conserving Church, would excel exceedingly, if they reclaimed these lost structures of responsibility and accountability.

Accountability structures need to have reinforcement mechanisms to succeed. In psychology, classical conditioning comes when someone develops a drive to do something because it is rewarding, or to stay away from certain practices, because they would be punished. In this conditioning, once a behaviour forms, it sticks. A conserving Church would succeed in its goal to shine God's light, if it nurtured a system where conservation activities, are rewarded, and destructive habits are punished. The church can only execute these measures among their members. Among the Yatta people of Kenya, a Christian denomination called Christian Impact Mission (CIM) established a mechanism where a tree would be planted for every birth by members of their church, and a wedding could only be officiated in a church, if the groom meets the condition of digging a water conservation pan, known as *silanga*. This reward and punishment mechanism help nurture a culture where members of Christ's body, together as a community, makes it a habit to participate in conservation measures.

Responsibility and accountability will be successful, if monitoring and evaluation mechanisms are put in place. Learned behavior would develop into a habit, if necessary, measures are put in place to support the change. A committed church, in my view, would become the best entity to play this role. A denomination in Yatta Kenya did this as part of their ministry. A group of adherents would be trained on a certain task, for example soil conservation technique. Then when they meet at home for prayer fellowships, the church leaders would ask the members of this group to hold their prayer fellowship next to where the initiative was implemented. First, the member would be given time to explain what was done, how it was done, and the challenges and successes observed in doing so. Then these members would pray and do a Bible study, that would also motivate them in some way, for example learning about the value of hard work.

## LOVE FOR KNOWLEDGE

In the book of Hosea 4:6, God laments that his people were perishing for lack of knowledge. God said his people did not have understanding. God's people would fail in their leadership and shining the light mandate, if they did not have the right knowledge and information necessary for carrying out God's tasks. There is a demand for thorough, qualified, and authoritative theological development in Kenya. Most of Christians are not even aware of what is expected of them and cannot be held accountable for their practices. The church generally does not have sufficient theological information in this area. Many Bible colleges do not have course on creation care. Pastors are trained in other aspects of theology such as hamartiology, Christology, ecclesiology, eschatology, but there is nothing on creation care. The Cape Town Convention offered four areas of possible theological work:

a) An integrated theology of creation care that can engage seminaries, Bible colleges and others to equip pastors to disciple their congregations.

b) A theology that examines humanity's identity as both embedded in creation and yet possessing a special role toward creation.

c) A theology that challenges current prevailing economic ideologies in relation to our biblical stewardship of creation.

d) A theology of hope in Christ and his Second Coming that properly informs and inspires creation care.[6]

Knowledge is said to be power, and when someone has knowledge and power, they also have influence. Shining God's light in the community requires important information of what works well, and the best science for performing things. The love for knowledge could be seen in missionary churches, which made it a priority to open-up schools, so that when children were learning about God, they could also learn math and science, together in the same place. The modern church could still use the same reasoning to develop a passion for the love of knowledge. In my observation, the Church in Kenya could stimulate its members to love and seek knowledge related to food, conservation, high value farming, innovation, sustainable energy, and development.

Knowledge about food production in an efficient way is very crucial for Christians in Kenya to have. Availability of technical information is instrumental in adoption of new farming initiatives. The colonial kind of farming, where machines ripped the ground with vigor and quaeks, has been adopted continually by many Kenyans. People grew with an understanding that the bigger

---

6. Cape Town Commitment, 6.

the machine, the better the produce. Over time however, and especially in the recent decades, soil has become "too tired" to sustain farming, irrespective of whether they are ripped and broken several times by heavy machinery. Well-connected farmers have even moved into the forest, to remove century old indigenous trees and convert the forests into farmlands. This too has been productive, but for few years. In my view, many people lack the knowledge and the science of crop production. Information on how to produce more from less land, how to build soil fertility, how to minimize soil erosion, and how to fix nitrogen into the soil naturally, is of great importance.

Christians in Kenya thus need information on how to exercise sustainable farming practices. Conservation farming involves practices that limit degradation and encourage rejuvenation and revitalization of soil. It includes practices such as minimal soil disturbance through zero or minimal rip tillage, mulching of the soil, rotation cropping, and use of natural ways of soil fertilization. It is understood that when soil is exposed to the sun, nitrogen tend to evaporate, making the soil to lose what is of great importance in its fertility quotient. Crops that fix nitrogen into the soil are grown periodically, and soil erosion is minimized completely. The basic goal of these principles is to help restore the overall health of soil thereby leading to increased, sustainable and healthy crop production. In the long run, it is hoped that due to undisturbed soil, insects such as earthworm will begin their work in the soil and with all these combinations of practices, soil gets restored and can be help in the production of food.

In conservation farming, standard management practice is maintained, so that wastes are minimized. Thus, weeding is done in the right time, and spacing of crops follow a well-researched guideline for maximum production. Burning of crop residue or of leaves and grass is strongly prohibited. This is because fire ravages the materials that could have been used in healing the soil. Leaves are left to decompose to give humus to the soil thus benefitting plants. If land is left to follow through this process for a long time, even degraded soil becomes rejuvenated. Furthermore, covered

# The Conserving Church in Kenya

soil is hard to be eroded, have minimal loss of moisture, have improved infiltration of water, and improved water holding capacity. Wendel Berry once connected very well the aspect of mulching and Christian faith:

> When I was there the cover crop was coming up to safeguard the ground over the winter. I looked for marks of erosion. There was none. It is possible, I think to say that this is a Christian agriculture, formed upon the understanding that it is sinful for people to misuse or destroy what they did not make.[7]

Berry's observation is a clear demonstration of how Christians can tangibly show that they are God's stewards. Similarly, the principle not to plough, especially as it is done in Kenya is because it is injurious to the soil. Tilling the soil destroys soil structure, organisms, and nutrients, leading to erosion, evaporation, infertility.

One boost that rejuvenated soil does to a community, is that it helps the poor to be able to produce food even from soil that have not been applied granular fertilizers. In many countries in the world, farming is gradually becoming a vocation for the rich and the politically connected. The poor cannot afford the machinery and the fertilizers. Yet they need food. The soils have become degraded due to farming methods and "too tired" to be useful. George Washington Carver avers:

> The farmer whose soil produces less every year is unkind to it in some way; that is, he is not doing what he should; he is robbing it of some substance it must have, and he becomes, therefore, a soil robber rather than a progressive farmer. We must enrich our soil every year instead of merely depleting it. It is fundamental that nature will drive away those who sin against it.[8]

Presbyterian Eco-Justice Task Force, presents typical situation in the world nowadays:

---

7. Berry, *The Unsettling of America*, 213.
8. Carver, *Soil*, 1.

"Green Revolution," for example, on which the final verdict is not in, developed modern varieties of grain far more productive than traditional varieties, and greatly enhanced the yields in countries such as India and Mexico. But those yields depended upon heavy inputs of synthetic fertilizer and pesticides, with increased mechanization of agriculture. Small farmers who could not afford the necessary investments lost their farms; some became landless peasants; some flocked to cities looking for jobs that were not there. In some places there was more hunger than before; and the modern methods of farming frequently degraded the natural fertility of the soil thereby increasing farmers' dependence on the inevitably more expensive and less available inputs from fossil fuels.[9]

The task of rejuvenating the soil should thus become a priority for a Christian. This require commitment, especially with a view of bringing God glory restoring one's farm to be like the Garden of Eden.

It is important for the Church to show concern for agricultural farms. The Sabbath principle prescribed in Torah predetermined how agricultural practices would be carried out. Israelites were expected to carry on their work and Sabbath rest seven years seven times. This will take 49 years. In the fiftieth year, they would all leave the land for a whole year to rest. This was the Jubilee year. The jubilee, according to Leviticus 25:23–28, is God's provision, given in order that the divine ownership of the land is respected and maintained. The idea behind leaving the land to rest was threefold: to leave the land to rejuvenate, to care for the poor and wild animals, and to teach Israelites that sustenance and blessings come from God; even when the land had been left untended. Presbyterian Eco-Justice Task Force indicates that God's intention was for the long-term sustenance of the land for all the people, together with the other creatures.[10] It is here shown clearly that God was

9. Presbyterian Eco-Justice Task Force, *Keeping and Healing the Creation*, 53.

10. Ibid., 47.

## The Conserving Church in Kenya

concerned about the land all along, prescribing specific actions for its treatment. Farming God's Way developed by Brian Oldrieve who first pioneered the practice on Hinton estate in Zimbabwe, beginning with a small piece of land, gradually adding the size, so that he eventually cropped 3,500 hectares. Grant Dryden has also contributed immensely in the development of this practice. Farming God's Way seeks to present God as central in the entire farming practice. The intention is to demonstrate the love for God in obedience, and the love for others in producing more food. This idea is based on interpretation of Genesis 2:8–9, which reads:

> Now the Lord God had planted a garden in the east in Eden; and there he put the man he had formed. And the Lord made all kinds of trees grow out of the ground— trees that were pleasing to the eye and good for food.[11]

The connection of farming to God presents farming, not just as an ordinary vocation, but noble. Sorley observes that it brings tremendous meaning and dignity to the realm of agriculture. Furthermore, the possibility that Farming God's Way can provide something like the proverbial Promised Land flowing with milk and honey, and with God watching over it from the beginning of the year to its end, is even more exciting.

Farming God's Way is established against the backdrop of failing agriculture in the world. Agriculture in the world, among the poor, is dependent on rainfall. Unfortunately, rainfall in the recent decades has become increasingly erratic, unpredictable and unreliable. Farmers no longer base their farming on any calendar, and crop failure is becoming a routine. Rising population, rising food costs and aging farmer community as young people move to the city, all cloud the situation further.

According Farming God's Way founders, the fact that God is the first farmer, means that the entire idea and purpose of farming is with him. Farming according to God should therefore be based on God's principles. Farming God's Way seeks to bring biblical injunctions and commitment for agricultural stewardship with

11. New International Version

practical principles on the farm which brings restoration and healing to the soil and resulting in improved crop production. It is believed that increased production gives God glory and providence to humanity.[12]

## SOCIAL TRANSFORMATION FOR CHRISTIANS IN KENYA

The church cannot become the light, unless it is transformed within itself to reflect God. The church should look like God in its values for industriousness, cultivation of good work ethic, and its love for contentment, and not materialism.

a. Love for industriousness and not pleasure

The Church has an opportunity to cause transformation, based on its familiarity and potential to transform existing cultures of the people of Kenya. There is a growing concern about Kenya's love of pleasure and irresponsible behavior. This is an opportunity for the Church, which is a hospital for sinners, to transform people in their conduct. In 2012, the municipal council of Eldoret said that wheat and maize farmers were losing thousands of shillings to prostitutes in Eldoret town. These farmers from Uasin Gishu and neighbouring districts became victims organized prostitutes travelling from Central province, strategically to prey on vulnerable farmers who had cash money from crop sale. According to Elizabeth Kibii, (Municipal Council's social services chairperson), complaints of loss of money in those situations had become rampant, with individual farmers losing as much as Sh500,000 in a day.[13] During the same period, similar cases were reported in Narok County. Julius Sigei's article in the East African Standard newspaper, reported of cases where farmers were swindled by prostitutes immediately after selling their wheat. Victims of such

12. Sorley, *Christ and Creation*, 2009.
13. Kibii. "Farmers Losing Their Money to Prostitutes In Kenya," 3.

atrocities usually suffer psychologically for many years, and some may not even return home due to disgrace. Their families usually end up as beggars, raising poverty level in the society even higher. A situation like this is reported in Ethiopia where farmers who were supported by Non-Governmental Organizations to do farming, ended up abusing alcohol, falling in the traps of prostitutes, or going gambling, making the situations in their families even worse.

### b. Positive work ethic

Environmental restoration activities are often physical exercises such as planting trees, building gabions, digging water pans to hold water, planting vetiver grass, applying mulch on the farm to stop erosion and increase fertility. Environmental success in degraded pieces of lands cannot happen, unless people develop a positive work ethic and a desire to "soil their hands." In the modern Kenya, a growing number of people do not have the right understanding of work. To them, a good work is a "white collar" job, which involves going to an office, which has a computer and a revolving chair. When people fail to get good grades in school, theyare assumed to become farmers. A parent would normally be heard challenging their school going children to work hard in school, or they would spend the rest of their lives in the farm touching the soil. School punishment for poor performers in academic fields, is normally related to digging out stumps, weeding maize, collecting leaves, and burning grass. It is so ironical that teachers teach about environmental stewardship, and the value of a good environment, but only ask the ill-behaved students to do those environmental related duties, as part of their punishment. Christians in Kenya, need to take up this situation as an opportunity to bring change. This requires churches to adopt and speak well of physical work, as something noble, for surely it is. A careful study of Genesis 1 and 2 shows God working, and on the 7th day resting. God plants trees, plants a garden, "soils his hands" to create Adam, and so forth. Christians need to take up the role of motivating their adherents to love to work, and to have a good understanding of work. In fact, Paul in the book of II Thessalonians, teach Christians that they should work, or else they should not eat.

### c. Individualized economic success

Conservation of environment should not lose the beautiful aspect of individual economic success of the participant. Change management related to environmental adaptation happens better when those adaptation initiatives are linked to direct individualized economic success. The idea that someone will benefit personally, for example gain profit for his family by participating in environmental stewardship will be something that attracts many people. I visited a group of bee keepers in Mount Kenya in 2013. I heard their success stories in being able to protect a section of the forest from being destroyed by corrupt officials and hungry neighbouring communities. Their great motivation, in my own judgement, was linked to their bee business. They had hanged their hives in the forest, and would harvest honey periodically, and sell as an organized group. These sales brought them significant amount of monetary profits, that they would be able to pay school fees for their children and buy food. I also attended an open day meeting in Nairobi at the A Rocha organization in Karen and listened to beautiful stories about conservation of Arabuko Sokoke forest in the Kenyan coast. The success was also linked to an ASSET program, where the community would benefit (individually) by having school fees for their children paid by A Rocha. In exchange, the community would cease any destructive activity, and would even prevent other people from doing so. The beautiful story I heard, was that Arabuko Sokoke forest was successfully coming back to life.

## d. Contentment not Materialism

The Church needs to fight the growing spirit of consumerism. Calvin DeWitt observes that there is a growing insatiable need in the whole world to consume. People always want to beyond the limits God has established.[14] The need for stewardship to train the society to see the prudence of refraining from consuming more than what is needed, and the reason to avoid following the relentless pursuit of luxuries is now in demand more than ever.[15] DeWitt avers that religion of high quality restores the ability of people and society to master themselves against unhealthy cravings, and instead revitalizes values and beliefs that bring respect for God and creation.[16]

The Bible deals with the subject of 'materialistic gluttony,' and offers direction for dealing with people with insatiable lusts for wealth. It does this by laying rules and procedures for conducting oneself, where the underlying principles are always concern for others rather than self. For example, the Sabbath rest of land and people given in Exodus 20:8–11, which is rarely practiced in the modern world, was to control people's unyielding desire for more and more wealth. People could only produce for so long and leave the land to rest in the seventh year (Leviticus 25:4). The people were supposed to refrain from attending their farms in this seventh year.

It is in this principle that we also understand God's concern for the poor and aliens (people who did not own land). The care of the land, and the rights of the poor and those in need were at the center of God's command. During this seventh year, the poor and the aliens would harvest free whatever grew naturally in the field. Adequate food was regarded as a God-given right for everyone. The poor people were allowed to feed on grapes in a neighbor's vineyard, or to pluck grain when passing by a field (Deuteronomy 23:24–25). Owners were urged to allow those in need to glean the leftovers from their harvest (Gnanakan 2004, 59). Wild animals

---

14. DeWitt, *Caring for Creation*, 34.
15. Acton Institute, *Environmental Stewardship*, 53.
16. DeWitt, *Caring for Creation*, 25.

would also benefit. The Israelites would record no harvest every seventh year, irrespective of owning chunks of land or being poor. The land would also rest, at least from the incessant farmer, who always wanted to work it every year (See also Exodus 23:10–13; Lev 25–26). The church can influence people in Kenya to stop this gluttony of wealth. It is this gluttony that makes the capitalist class to destroy the forest instead of planting trees. The destruction of Mau forest was originally designed to provide habitat for few poor people during the time of President Daniel Arap Moi. The people that ended up benefitting from the forest were rich government officials, some of whom did not even know the specific location of their farms, or where their boundaries were. As a result, trees were destroyed carelessly within a short period of time, to create more space for farming.

This spirit of consumerism, which was a product of capitalism, is one of the one of the greatest monsters which humanity faces today. The God given resources are exploited with blatant insult to the giver, and utter disregard of tomorrow's generation. One of the commitments of Cape Town Convention was to a simple lifestyle Christians can change the world if they recognized the impact they would have by personally and collectively, living within limited and proper boundaries of natural resources provided by God, and to engage further in the restoration and conservation.[17] This includes a well-thought-out economic plan that puts into consideration sustainable development in relation to energy, natural resource management, infrastructure, waste disposal, *et cetera*.

One of the chief motivations for materialism is corruption. Eunice Kamaara argues that capitalism is to blame for the rampant cases of corruption in Kenya. According to Eunice Kamaara (2000), capitalism is one public economic perspective that has in a greater sense been detrimental to the wellbeing of the people. Capitalism is responsible for the current obsession with private accumulation of wealth at the expense of the public good, a practice that exacerbated destruction of natural resources. Kamaara opines that the Church in Kenya has an important role to play to serve as

17. Cape Town Committment, 6.

the conscience of the nation. This includes confronting the government and other public policy leaders to prioritize in the welfare of the public, especially the poor, and not the rich well-connected individuals. She asserts:

> In addition to the fact that corruption distorts economic incentives and thus discourages wealth creation, it exacerbates the problem of income and wealth inequality. Corruption tends to transfer income from the poor and concentrates it in the hands of the rich and politically powerful. In addition, it distorts public policy outcomes and makes it difficult for the state to deal effectively with poverty. It is not unusual for resources destined for the poor to end up in the hands of rich bureaucrats and politicians. The church, serving as an advocate for the poor, can insist on more transparency in government, a process that can significantly reduce the incidence of mismanagement and improve the functioning of programs to aid the poor.[18]

This assertion by Kamaara shows that enormous role that Christians have in the society in relation to public policy and corruption. Although Kamaara does not discuss here the role of the church in environmental policies, it could be inferred, since involvement in public policy cuts across the social needs.

## CONCLUSION

In this chapter, I have pinpointed various activities that the church in Kenya should consider letting their members participate in. The church needs to marshal its forces to conduct campaigns on creation care. It should not be a task of few informed people being funded by foreign organizations, usually meeting in hotel conferences and taking tea. It should be a work of the whole church, and mobilization the whole society. It should be made to become like evangelism, where members of the church are encouraged to make

18. Kamaara, "The Role of the Christian Church in Socioeconomic and Political Development in Kenya," 165.

## Christian Faith and Environmental Stewardship

use of their varied talents. The Church can also make creation care a mission work, targeting the unreached people groups for the whole gospel (including creation care). The Cape Town Convention stated that "we encourage the Church to promote 'environmental missions' as a new category within mission work (akin in function to medical missions).[19]

The Church needs to be creative to safeguard and enhance the creation. A good steward is careful neither to leave the resources entrusted to him to lie idle or to fail to produce their proper fruit, nor does he destroy them. Instead, the good steward uses them, develops them, secures and increases the resource, so that he may enjoy his livelihood and provide for the good of his family and his descendants.[20]

A Chinese proverb states that the best time to plant a tree is 20 years ago. The second-best time is now. The environmental situation in Kenya now is like an analogy used by Ed Brown of a leaking ship. In an ordinary ship, there are many people with different duties. Some are cooks, others captains, others, security personnel, others cleaners, and still others engineers. If there is a leak, a dangerous one, all activities become temporarily useless, until the problem is fixed. In this analogy, Brown observes that the problem with the environmental 'ship' has to be fixed or nothing else will matter, because the ship has a problem, and if not fixed, it will not reach the port.[21]

Above all, the church needs to promote obedience to God. Environmental success can only be successful, if God is in the picture. Only when can God truly forgive the people and heal the land. God makes it clear in the book of his blessings and more blessings go hand in hand with reciprocated faithfulness. Deuteronomy presents a situation where Israelites' ongoing occupancy of the land given to them as a blessing, depended on their moral behaviour and their observance of the law.[22] Environmental stew-

---

19. Cape Town Commitment, 6.
20. Acton Institute, *Environmental Stewardship*, 39–40.
21. Brown, *Our Father's World*, 91.
22. Gnanakan, *Responsible Stewardship of God's Creation*, 62.

## The Conserving Church in Kenya

ardship in Kenya can be done in the same way. The church needs to influence the society to understand that good environment is given by God, and a degraded environment is a punishment for idolatry and injustice. The people can get blessings of rain and blessed soil when they detach themselves and their society from evil. The book of II Chronicles 7:14 provides clear direction of what God's people need to do to get God's blessings:

> If my people, who are called by my name, will humble themselves and pray and seek my face and turn from their wicked ways, then will I hear from heaven and will forgive their sin and will heal their land.[23]

This verse shows that the healing of the land comes as the end-product of a process that begins with individual people called the "people of God." This passage clearly demonstrates that environmental stewardship should first be viewed as the work of God's people. These people, acting out of love of God and their neighbours need to wake up with the realization that environmental healing is a task waiting for them to perform. Upon realization of this task, these people of God need to humble themselves and pray. Humility is an important virtue in seeking God. Humility is the attitude of saying "I do not call the shots; I depend on someone else." Spiritual matters demand spiritual perspective. The fact that God can heal the land is a spiritual matter that deserves spiritual attention. The spiritual people praying to God should first have the attitude that everything depends on God. This humility is best illustrated by the life of Jesus himself, whom Apostle Paul refers to have been God in the very nature but chose to take the nature of a servant. This humility of God-incarnate, to accomplish a bigger task is what God's people are expected to emulate. The humility and prayer are not enough. God's people need to turn from their wicked ways. According to prophet Amos, Israel's wickedness could be summarized as idolatry and injustice. God's people therefore need to turn away from worshipping anything other than God, and from all kinds of injustice to their neighbours. If all of

23. New International Version.

God's people do these, God will surely forgive people and heal the land. A healed land is a blessed land. It will be a land teeming with animals and plants; fresh air and clean water; a land that is productive, so that there is no want.

Naim Stifan Ateek asserts that God's dealing with Israel, including the land the He gave them, was not for that group of people alone. God chose one nation to be a model of how He would have liked the entire humanity to be related to Him. They should be perceived as a paradigm, a model, for God's concern for every people and every land. All people are supposed to obey God's commands, and to keep justice and love in the land, so that they can enjoy long life in the land.[24]

---

24. Ateek in Gnanakan, *Responsible Stewardship of God's Creation*, 57.

# Bibliography

Ackello-Ogutu, C. "'Livestock production', In Environmental Change and Dryland Management in Machakos District, Kenya 1930–90 ." Edited by M. Tiffen. (Overseas Development Institute) Working Paper no. 55 (1991): 45–89.

Acton Institute. *Environmental Stewardship in the Judeo-Christian Tradition: Jewish, Catholic and Protestant Wisdom on the Environment.* Grand Rapids, Michigan: Acton Institute, 2007.

Attfield, R. *The Ethics of Environmental Concern.* New York, NY: Columbia University Press, 1983.

Barnes. "Barnes Notes on the Bible." http://biblehub.com/commentaries/genesis/1-28.htm. Not dated.

Basher, R., and S Briceño S. "Climate and Disaster Risk Reduction in Africa," in Pak Sum Low, ed., Climate Change and Africa. Cambridge: Cambridge University Press, 2005.

Bohemen, Samira van. "Divergent Religious Conceptions of Nature: Dualism and Holism: A Study on Religion and Environmental Concern in the Netherlands." Thesis. Erastus University, Rotterdam, 2010.

Brown, Edward. *Our Father's World.* South Hadley, Massachusetts: Doorlight, 2006.

Brown, Edward R. *When Heaven and Nature Sing: Exploring God's Goals for His people and His World.* South Hadley, Massachusetts: Doorlight, 2012.

Calvin, John. "First book of Moses called Genesis" in Craig Sorley, Commentaries on the Christ and Creation. Kijabe: Care of Creation Kenya, 2009.

———. N.Y. Institutes of Christian Religion, Vol I, xiv 2; xiv 22. . Vols. I, xiv 2; xiv 22.

Campbell, C. *The Easternization of the West: A Thematic Account of Cultural Change in the Modern Era.* London: Paradigm Publishers, 2008.

Cape Town Commitment. 2010.

Christian, Diana Leafe. "Accountability and Consequences." Communities 117 (2003): 16–19.

DeWitt, Calvin. *Caring for Creation: Responsible Stewardship of God's Handiwork.* Baker, 1998.

## Bibliography

Dyke, Fred van, David C. Mahan, Joseph K. Sheldon, and Raymond H. Brand. *Redeeming Creation: The Biblical Basis of Environmental Stewardship*. Downers Grove, Illinois: Intervarsity, 1996.

Gnanakan, Ken. *Responsible Stewardship of God's Creation*. Bangalore, India: Theological Book Trust, 2004.

Haar, Gerrie Ter, and Stephen Ellis. "The Role of Religion in Development: Towards a New Relationship between the European Union and Africa." *The European Journal of Development Research 18(3)* (2006): 351–367.

Hastenrath, S. *Climate Dynamics of the Tropics*. Dortrecht, Netherlands: Kluwer, 1991.

Holling, C. S. "Resilience and Stability of Ecological Systems." *Annual Review of Ecology and Systematics 4* (1973): 1–23. Accessed 12 June 2018. https://doi.org/10.1146/annurev.es.04.110173.000245.

Huang, J, C. Pray, and S Rozelle. "Enhancing the Crops to Feed the Poor." *Nature 481* (2002): 678–684.

Ilo, Stan Chu. *The Chuch and Development in Africa: Aid and Development from the Perspective of Catholic Social Ethics*. Eugene, Oregon: Pickwick, 2011.

Jendia, Catherine. "Leadership, Accountability, and Integrity: An African." *International Journal of Sciences: Basic and Applied Research (IJSBAR) 24 (2)* (2015): 164–176.

Kenya Forest Working Group. 2006.

Kibii, Elizabeth. n.d. "Farmers Losing Their Money To Prostitutes In Kenya." http://news.naij.com/13656.html., Not dated.

Land, Richard D. and Louis A. Moore. *The Earth Is the Lord's: Christian and the Environment*. Nashville, Tennessee: Broadman, 1992.

Lane, Dermot A. "Anthropological and Theological Reflections on Laudato Si'." In *Laudato Si' An Irish Response: Essays on the Pope's Letter on the Environment*, by Sean, Ed. Mcdonagh, 31–54. Dublin, Ireland: Veritas, 2017.

Leber, Jessica, "How Farmers in Kenya Might Adapt to Climate Change." SCIEN: Scientific American (Leber, J. (2010). How Farmers in Kenya Might Adapt to Climate Change. *SCIEN: Scientific American* (2010): 12–24.

Lezberg, S. L. "Political ecology and resource management: An examination of response to soil erosion in Machakos District, Kenya. M.A. thesis, Clark University, Worcester, MA." 1988

Lowe, Ben.. *Green Revolution: Coming Together to Care for Creation*. Downers Grove, Illinois: IVP, 2009.

Luganda, P. "Africa and Climate Change: Bringing Science and Development together through Original News and Analysis." *SciDev.Net.*, 2008.

Marlow, Hillary. *The Earth is the Lord's: A Biblical Response to Environmental Issues*. Cambridge: Grove, 2008.

Masika, Titus. *Mindset Change for Community Transformation*. Nairobi: Sahel, 2016.

Mburu, Benson Kamau, James Biu Kung'u, and John Njagi Muriuki. "Climate change adaptation strategies by small-scale in Yatta District Kenya."

*Bibliography*

African Journal of Environmental Science and Technology 9 (9) (2015): 712–722.

Mogaka, Hezron, Samuel Gichere, Richard Davis, and Rafik Hirji. Climate Variability and Water Resources DEGRADATION in Kenya: Improving Water Resources Development and Management. *World Bank Working Papers*, 2005.

Munyao, Carol Munini, Fred Muisu, Jacob Mbego, Francis Mburu, and Peter Sirma. 2013. "Influence of Land Size on Adoption of Jatropha Curcas in Yatta." *Journal of Natural Sciences Research 3 (4)* (2013): 42–50.

Nash, Roderick Frazier. *The Rights of Nature: A History of Environmental Ethics*. Madison: University of Wisconsin Press, 1989.

Ngigi, Stephen N. "Review of Irrigation Development in Kenya." Edited by Herbert G. Blank, Clifford M. Mutero and Hammond Murray-Rust. Colombo: International Water Management Institute, 2002.

Oinas-Kukkonen, Harri. "Behavior Change Support Systems: A Research Model and Agenda." *Persuasive Technology* (2010): 4–14.

O'Keefe, John J. "Creation, Incarnation, and Resurrection." In *God, Creation, and Climate Change: A Catholic Response to the Environmental Crisis*, by Richard W. Ed. Miller, 49–68. Maryknoll, NY: Orbis Books, 2010.

Peberdy, J. R. *Machakos District Gazetteer, Machakos District Office*. Nairobi: Department of Agriculture, 1958.

Piper, John. *The Pleasures of God*. Sisters, Oregon: Multinomah Publishers, Inc, 2000.

Presbyterian Eco-Justice Task Force. *Keeping and Healing the CREATION*. Louisville, KY: Presbyterian Church, 1989.

Republic of Kenya. *Kenya*. Kenya National Bureau of Statistics, 2009.

Rignot, Eric and Pannir Kanagaratnam. "Changes in the Velocity and Structure of the Greenland Ice Sheet." *Science 311* (2006): 986–990.

Rolston, H. III. "Caring for Nature." *Environmental Values 15 (3)* (2006): 307–314.

Sorley, Craig. *Christ and Creation*. Kijabe: Care of Creation Kenya, 2009.

Stewart, Nola. "Caring for God's Creation." May: 1–30, 2010. http://www.confessingcongregations.com/uploads/acc_caring_for_the_creation_2nd_ed.pdf.

Stewart, Ruth Goring. *Environmental Stewardship*. Downers Grove, Illinois: Intervarsity, 1990.

Tacket, Del. "What's a Christian Worldview?" Focus on the Family, 2006. https://www.focusonthefamily.com/faith/christian-worldview/whats-a-christian-worldview/whats-a-worldview-anyway.

Taskforce to Inquire into Forest Resource Management and Logging Activities in A REPORT ON FOREST RESOURCES MANAGEMENT AND LOGGING ACTIVITIES IN KENYA. Nairobi: Republic of Kenya, 2018.

Tiffen, Michael Mortimore, and Francis Gichuki. *More People Less Erosion*. Nairobi: Act, 1994.

## Bibliography

United Nations Development Program. http://hdr.undp.org/en/humandev., 2018.

United Nations Environmental Program. "Environment in Kenya." Nairobi, 2002.

United Nations Environmental Program, *Kenya: Atlas of our Changing Environment*. Nairobi: United Nations Environmental Program, 2009.

Verbrugge, Verlyn D. Ed., *New International DICTIONARY of New Testament Theology*. Grand Rapids, Michigan: Zondervan, 2000.

World Commission on Environment and Development. "Report of the World Commission on Environment and Development: Our Common Future," 1987. www.documents.net/weed-ocf.htm.

Made in United States
North Haven, CT
23 April 2022